Black Women and the Struggle against Apartheid in South Africa

Black Women and the Struggle against Apartheid in South Africa

A Thesis Submitted in Partial Fulfillment of the Requirements for the Degree of Master of Arts

Oyibo H. Afoaku

Copyright © 2023 by Oyibo H. Afoaku.

Library of Congress Control Number:		2022924096
ISBN:	Hardcover	978-1-6698-6132-4
	Softcover	978-1-6698-6131-7
	eBook	978-1-6698-6130-0

All rights reserved. No part of this book may be reproduced or transmitted in any form or by any means, electronic or mechanical, including photocopying, recording, or by any information storage and retrieval system, without permission in writing from the copyright owner.

Any people depicted in stock imagery provided by Getty Images are models, and such images are being used for illustrative purposes only.
Certain stock imagery © Getty Images.

Print information available on the last page.

Rev. date: 12/29/2022

To order additional copies of this book, contact:
Xlibris
844-714-8691
www.Xlibris.com
Orders@Xlibris.com

848576

CONTENTS

Abstract vii
Acronyms ix
Acknowledgments xi

Chapter 1: Introduction 1

Chapter 2: Black Women In Precolonial South Africa 15
    Introduction 16
    Initiation Rites and Gender Roles in Precolonial Society 18
    Gender Relations in Precolonial Society 23
    Conclusion 30

Chapter 3: Black Women And Apartheid Laws 32
    Introduction 33
    Black Women and White Domination Before Apartheid 44
    Black Women and Apartheid Laws 53
    Conclusion 72

Chapter 4: Black Women's Response To Apartheid 74
    Introduction 75
    Profiles 81
        Winnie Mandela 81
        Nontsikelelo Albertina Sisulu 85
        Emma Mashinini 89
        Thenjiwe Mtintso 95
    Conclusion 100

Chapter 5: Conclusion: Black Women In Post-Apartheid
     South Africa 104
  Introduction 105
  From Apartheid to Multiracial Democracy 106
  Black Women and the 1996 Constitution 112
  Conclusion 116

Bibliography 123
Index 137

ABSTRACT

TRADITIONALLY, ACADEMIC DISCUSSION about apartheid has been dominated by the power struggles between Black and White males within the framework of an oppressive system that was based on patriarchy and White racial superiority. Consequently, Black women's experiences and contributions in the struggle against apartheid have not received the emphasis that they deserve in scholarly discussion of apartheid. This study represents an attempt to narrow this gap.

It is noteworthy that gender inequality was tolerated in precolonial South Africa. As evidenced by initiation ceremonies in precolonial South Africa, traditional processes of socialization were carefully designed to prepare male and female children for their future roles in the political, social, and economic dimensions of society as adults. Rapid changes took place in South Africa following the arrival of the Europeans in the late 1500s, especially with the establishment of the famous "service station" at the Cape of Good Hope in 1652. Specifically, the conditions of Black women were compounded by these changes as native South Africans progressively lost control of their destiny with the subsequent influx of European immigrants, the Boer Trek, the discovery of gold and diamonds in the second half of the nineteenth century, imposition of British rule at the end of the South African War of 1899–1902 and, especially, imposition of apartheid from 1948 through 1994.

Apartheid had multiple implications for Black women; it had negative impacts on their relationships with Black men, their relationships with other women, and particularly with the White minority regime. Under apartheid rule, Black women were subjected to threefold discrimination based on class, gender, and race. Through their collective actions and the leadership provided by individuals, Black women's struggles against apartheid had a powerful impact on the feminist movement in South Africa. More importantly, they made remarkable contributions toward the collapse of the apartheid system and the emergence of multiracial democracy in South Africa in 1994 through collaborations with anti-apartheid groups within and outside the country. One of the several challenges facing post-apartheid South Africa is related to translating the lofty provisions of its democratic constitution in ways that will significantly improve the status of women, especially Black women.

ACRONYMS

ANC	African National Congress
ANCWL	African National Congress Women's League
AZAPO	Azanian People's Organization
CCAWUSA	Commercial, Catering, and Allied Workers Union of South Africa
COSATU	Congress of South African Trade Unions
DPSC	Detainees Parents' Support Committee
ECC	End Conscription Campaign
FSAW	Federation of South African Women
NNC	South African Native National Congress
NUDW	National Union of Distributive Workers
PAC	Pan African Congress
SACP	South African Communist Party
SAIC	South African Indian Congress
SASO	South African Student Organization
UDF	United Democratic Front
UNESCO	United Nations Educational, Scientific, and Cultural Organization
WWI	World War I
WWII	World War II

ACKNOWLEDGMENTS

I AM ALWAYS GRATEFUL for the invaluable love and support I have received from my parents, Samuel Nweke and Victoria Obijele Akunkwo (Nnenne) Akpu. Their belief in equal educational opportunity for their sons and daughter, and their relentless support have encouraged me to believe that I could be whatever I want to be in life. I am deeply grateful to my husband, Dr. Osita G. Afoaku, and our four beautiful children—Mmachukwu Helisita, Nzubechukwu Nancy, Onyinyechukwu George, and Amalachukwu Karen Afoaku—for their love and encouragement during the difficult times.

Friends and relatives to whom I owe much gratitude for their support and encouragement include Nancy M. Collins-Warner, Herrick and Diane Garnsey, Dr. and Mrs. C. M. (Mike) and Julie Churchill, Dr. Beth Prinz, Marianne Dinges, Dorothy Mbanefo, Commy Ukaegbu, Dr. Asopuru Alajemba Okemgbo, and Dr. David L. Coon. My brothers and their families: F. B. O. and Ifeoma Eugenia, Chukwunwike Cyril and Nonyelum Winifred, Chukwunweuba Samuel, and Olisaemeka Charles Akpuenika. My thanks and love to Okey Patrick Nwafor, Roseline Mgbeagheliaku Ekweozor, and Elizabeth UcheChukwu Akpu.

My experience in completing this project would not have been as positive as it turned out to be without a very supportive thesis committee. I owe special gratitude to my adviser, Dr. Marshall Clough, for guiding and steering my research toward a successful end. I am particularly appreciative of his patience and thoroughness throughout the process. I am equally thankful to Dr. Janet Worrall and Dr. Ronald Edgerton for taking their time to review my work at various stages and for providing very constructive comments and suggestions.

CHAPTER 1

Introduction

The best would be to do what they do in Japan - move people with bullet trains into the (white) working areas by day and take them back to their homes at night In the tribal homelands. I don't see why this country can't do it; we've got the money. But, of course, this is a large country, so it would be more difficult. But this would be the ideal thing.[1]

—Gabrielle Malan

In June 1958 he was granted four days' permission to leave Johannesburg for us to get married - besides being an accused in the Treason Trial he was also banned - I insisted on getting married at home in Pondoland, because nothing could have pleased my father better and I wanted Nelson to see my background. It was an initiation for the kind of life we were heading for anyway because we had to dash back without even completing the usual marriage ceremony in the traditional manner.

---

1 Mrs. Gabrielle Malan in 1978, in June Goodwin, *Cry Amandla: South African Women and the Question of Power* (New York: Africana Publishing Company, 1984), 51. In 1978, June Goodwin, an American journalist, interviewed Mrs. Malan, the wife of Minister Malan of the three largest Dutch Reformed Churches in South Africa and one of the architects of apartheid. Malan is a popular Afrikaner name. Mrs. Malan was a staunch supporter of apartheid and came from a "mixed marriage." Her mother was Irish and her father was Afrikaner. It was ironic that she supported a system which forbade mixed marriages.

After the marriage in my home, we were supposed to then get married in his home as well. As far as the elders in the family are concerned, we haven't finished getting married to this day.[2]

—Winnie Mandela

We waited outside the court where they would be driven to Pretoria Central Prison, to wave goodbye to them for the last time. We were in the midst of this huge crowd - I held Zeni's hand and Zindzi was on my arm - when someone grasped my shoulder. I turned and what do I see? A huge policeman and he says: "Remember your permit! You must be in Johannesburg by twelve o'clock."[3]

—Winnie Mandela

HISTORICALLY, DOMINANT GROUPS have established legal/ideological frameworks to consolidate and legitimize their hegemonic status across societies. Given the centrality of such arrangements to the preservation of their power and privileges, there is usually no incentive to dismantle these until they are vigorously challenged by marginalized groups. The struggle to replace apartheid with a democratically elected regime in South Africa thus bears a close

---

2   Winnie Mandela, *Part of my Soul Went With Him,* edited by Anne Benjamin, adopted by Mary Benson (New York: W. W. Norton & Company, 1985), 60–61. In this biography, Mrs. Winnie Mandela shares her frustration with the apartheid system, which did not allow enough time to Mr. Nelson Mandela so that they could complete their marriage ceremonies according to their tradition and culture. Nelson was granted only four days' permission to leave Johannesburg for them to get married because he was an accused in the Treason Trial and was already banned. So, by implication, Mr. and Mrs. Mandela never had an opportunity to develop and enjoy a normal marital relationship because of the apartheid system.

3   Ibid., 81.

resemblance to the anti-colonial struggle in the rest of Africa and elsewhere.

While the liberation struggle in South Africa has received significant attention in scholarly discussions, there has been relatively little attempt to examine in detail the contributions of African women in this respect. On the one hand, the literature on South Africa tends to include passing references to the women's contributions to anti-apartheid resistance or to exclude them altogether. On the other hand, it is replete with references to the names of prominent African men and their roles in dismantling the apartheid regime. Consequently, little attention has been given to the fact that as double victims, not only did Black women suffer the debilitating effects of White racism and sexism but they were also confronted with gender-based discrimination by Black men throughout the years of resistance against apartheid. Notably, the tendency to marginalize Black women in the academic treatment of the anti-apartheid struggle forms part of a larger trend in anti-colonial discourse. The danger of this parochialism is twofold: by emphasizing only the racial foundation of the apartheid system in the historiography of the South African experience, scholars could become unsuspecting accomplices in concealing the patriarchal foundation of apartheid; more importantly, by minimizing the contributions of Black women toward the struggle against apartheid, we could potentially abet the marginalization of women in post-apartheid South Africa. After all, this is already happening in most of postcolonial Africa where, in spite of the women's contribution toward the effort to eradicate European domination, they have been generally denied those freedoms and privileges that they fought for while the men have controlled political and economic power.

The present work represents an attempt to bridge the gap in the academic treatment of the Black women's liberation struggle in South Africa. While not discounting the centrality of race to the formulation and implementation of apartheid laws, it attempts to draw attention to the uniqueness of Black women's experience with the apartheid regime by bringing into focus the combined impacts of racism and sexism on the latter during the years of anti-apartheid resistance.

It should be pointed out that race relations in South Africa had considerably deteriorated long before the formal adoption of the apartheid regime as a system of governance based on the principle of racial separation. Apartheid became the legal basis of public policy in South Africa in 1948 and remained in place until 1994 when Pretoria's White minority regime was replaced with a democratic Black majority regime. With the institutionalization of apartheid, Pretoria became the seat of the most notorious racist government in the twentieth century. Richard S. Willen describes apartheid South Africa as follows:

> South Africa is a racially segregated society. Its political, economic, and social institutions are founded upon the policy of apartheid. This means that race is the sole criterion for determining people's position in society: their rights, privileges, immunities, and opportunities. Participation in controlling political processes is reserved to whites. Position in the economy is also allocated in accordance with racial criteria. Socio-legal status is based on racial particularism and a person's membership in a racial group or category determines his place in society.[4]

South Africa's White minority enjoyed the political, economic, and social privileges of a newly industrialized society. At the same time, the Blacks who formed the majority of the country's population were denied all the privileges and human rights due to being citizens of a civilized society. Apartheid was the brainchild of the Afrikaners or Boers, who were the descendants of the Dutch settlers who first arrived in South Africa in 1652. The Dutch Reformed Church was the official religion of the apartheid regime. The Afrikaners based the apartheid system on

---

4   Richard S. Willen, "Normative Structure of South African Inequality," *Free Inquiry in Creative Sociology*, 10:1 (May 1982): 80.

a skewed doctrine supplied by the Dutch Reformed Church, according to which White rule in South Africa was consistent with "divine will" and was, therefore, unique on the basis of any human standard of wrong and right.[5]

Against this background, it should be noted that Black women fought side by side with their husbands and other relatives to dismantle apartheid. Prominent among these women were Mrs. Winnie Mandela, Mrs. Adelaide Joseph, Mama Dorothy, Mrs. Albertina Sisulu, Rita Ndzanga, and a host of others. It is also noteworthy that although the African National Congress was formed in 1912, it was not until 1943 that the ANC's new constitution extended its membership to women.[6] As will be shown later, it became necessary for Black women to found the ANC Women's League (ANCWL) after they were formally allowed to participate in the mainstream anti-apartheid organization. In a sense, therefore, Black South African women fought against three enemies: sexism as manifested in the attitudes of their male relatives and ANC policies; sexism and racism as manifested in the attitudes of White males and apartheid policies; and finally, racism and internalized sexism as manifested in the attitudes of White women who supported apartheid. For instance, Mrs. Malan, the wife of one of the architects of apartheid and minister of the Dutch Reformed Church, believed in apartheid and defended it with the conviction that the Afrikaners were destined to rule South Africa. Like most Afrikaner women, she supported their men, who were charged with the enforcement of racist policies designed to maintain Blacks and other non-White groups in a subordinate position. Among other factors, the unflinching support that Afrikaner women such as Mrs. Malan lent to apartheid played a significant part in concealing the fact that White hegemony in South Africa was, at the same time, driven by racial and gender prejudice.[7] Thus, by virtue of their race and gender, Black women were triple

---

5 Goodwin, *Cry Amandla*, 51–56.
6 Mandela, *Part of my Soul*, 106–111.
7 Goodwin, *Cry Amandla*, 51–61

victims. As a result of all of these policies, Black women were ultimately forced to remain at the bottom of the economic ladder as well.

Owing to the divisive strategy of the apartheid regime, it took six years after the inception of apartheid for South African women of different racial/ethnic backgrounds (Blacks, Colored, Indian, and a few liberal Whites) to appreciate the need for an umbrella organization that would serve as a political forum for addressing their common interests and objectives. On April 17, 1954, these women founded the Federation of South African Women (FSAW). This organization played an important role in the protest politics of the 1950s. For example, on August 9, 1956, about twenty thousand women of all races organized a peaceful and big demonstration in the Union Buildings in Pretoria.[8] As will be explained later, this event was of historical significance because, for the first time, the women of South Africa were able to establish a common agenda based on their appreciation of the intersection of race, class, and gender in apartheid South Africa. They also demonstrated to the Pretoria government and the international community that they were a power to be reckoned with in the struggle against apartheid. Prominent among these women was Mrs. Winnie Mandela, who was expecting her first baby at the time. Notably, Winnie was among the women arrested and detained for the march on Pretoria.

She was subsequently fired from her job because of her political views and activities. Nevertheless, Winnie remained a voice in the national liberation movement.[9]

As a system of oppression based on racial and gender prejudice, apartheid protected White women at the expense of Black women. Frequently, male relatives of Black women were taken away from them. Black women like Winnie Mandela suffered heavily as a result of prolonged separation from their spouses because the latter were serving long prison terms. Others suffered frequent separation from their

---

8   Lloys L. Frates, "Women in the South African National Liberation Movement, 1948–1960: An Historiographical Overview," *Ufahamu: Journal of the African Activist Association* v. 21, n. 1–2 (1993): 27–34.
9   Ibid., 27–34.

spouses who were hired by White employers as migrant workers. These women and the rest of their family members left behind by their male relatives were at the mercy of security agents who maintained constant surveillance on Black homelands. In addition, Black women suffered discrimination while serving as maids for white households or as Black workers supervised by White bosses. Black schoolchildren were forced to remain under the Bantu Education system, an inferior education system created and controlled by the apartheid regime for Black children.[10] Like other non-White persons, they faced the humiliation of carrying passes and being the subject of scrutiny on a daily basis and not to mention the random, unprovoked aggression by Whites of every status in their own country. For Black South African women, "There was much more at stake than simply the dignity of womanhood."[11] Apartheid provoked many Black women to resist racist and sexist policies in some passive ways while it forced others to adopt militant tactics like their men. For instance, as a matter of philosophy, the ANC adopted the policy of non-violence or passive resistance for about half a century but was forced to abandon it for military resistance in the early 1960s as the minority government continued to respond to peaceful demonstrations, protests, or gatherings with violence.[12]

At this juncture, it is important to mention that as soon as the Union was formed in 1910, South Africa began to undergo rapid changes, including the restriction of the movement of the natives. For instance, Black women's efforts to protest pass policy date back to 1913. As Julia Wells states,

---

10 Mandela, *Part of My Soul*, 112. Cock, Jacklyn, *Maids and Madams: A Study in the Politics of Exploitation* (Johannesburg: Raven Press, 1984), 26–86.
11 Julia C. Wells, "Why Women Rebel: a Comparative Study of South African Women's Resistance in Bloemfontein (1913) and Johannesburg (1958)," *Journal of Southern African Studies* v.10, n. 1 (1983): 55.
12 Ruth Mompati, "The Most Powerful Woman in the African National Congress" in Diana E. H. Russell, *Lives of Courage: Women For A New South Africa* (New York: Basic Books, Inc., Publishers, 1989), 118–120; Nelson Mandela, *Long Walk To Freedom: The Autobiography of Nelson Mandela* (Boston: Little, Brown and Company, 1994), 235–236, 280–281; Leo Kuper, *Passive Resistance in South Africa* (New Haven: Yale University Press, 1957), 9–10, 122–133.

As in 1913, the question of women's passes had already been hot political issue for several years prior to the passive resistance of 1958. The announcement in late 1955 that the government intended to start issuing passes to African women in 1956 tremendously boosted the enthusiasm and following of both the African National Congress Women's League (ANCWL) and the non-racial umbrella organization to which it belonged, the Federation of South Africa Women (FSAW). From then on, the ANCWL and FSAW successfully carried out an active campaign of public resistance to the very idea of passes for women.[13]

These women organized two large protests at the administrative buildings in Pretoria in 1954 and 1958 respectively, and a few other smaller protests. In addition, they initiated a program of political education designed to enlighten Black women about the need to resist pass laws. Their protest slowed down the government's effort at issuing passes to non-White South Africans. Specifically, the government initiated a new policy of issuing passes on a voluntary basis first in 1913 in Bloemfontein. Most of the women involved in the anti-pass protest were from Sophiatown, a Black residential area close to Johannesburg. During the 1958 protest, Black women from Sophiatown ignored police orders to disperse, and about one thousand of them were sent to jail. In response to this development, more women from Alexandria township to the north of Johannesburg joined the anti-pass protests as many of them were sent to jail as well.[14]

Obviously, these women did not embark on anti-pass protests to seek imprisonment but took things as they came. It is a great testimony to their courage that some of them refused to be bailed out of prison because they believed that they were fighting a just cause for which they were prepared to die. Their "obstinacy" brought about some

---

13 Ibid., 59.
14 Ibid., 58–59.

disagreements between the ANC male leaders and the female leaders. The men wanted their womenfolk to stop seeking the arrest and to start seeking bail so they would get out of prison. Unfortunately, the women's anti-pass campaign proved to be only a temporary success, and gradually African women were forced to accept passes reluctantly from the 1960s. This setback was due to two major factors: their inability to continue to resist or protest and their inability to resist pressures from some male leaders who did not want women to "get too involved" in the struggle against apartheid.[15] However, with the imprisonment, murder, and sending into exile of the male leaders, ANCWL and the FSAW leaders in Johannesburg were forced to embrace the fact that the struggle against White minority rule should transcend passive resistance. There was also a growing realization that in order for the struggle to achieve positive results, all segments of the non-White communities, including the women, should be allowed to make some contributions. When the ANC decided to abandon passive resistance in the 1950s, it was obvious that Black women could not be excluded from militant activism.

The above development was all the more predictable in view of the fact that apartheid policy included sexist laws such as the one that classified married women as minors. By implication, married Black women could not make use of their initiatives in relation to legal matters. For example, this law prohibited a married woman from signing legal documents such as a marriage certificate on behalf of her family. Given the fact that Black families were often separated or dismantled completely as a result of problems associated with apartheid policies, this law made life particularly difficult for Black women who were infantilized by the system. As will be explained in subsequent chapters, Black families were frequently broken up due to difficulties associated with the men's long and frequent absence from the home due to their decision to become migrant employees, or some other unfortunate situations like imprisonment, political exile, or even death in the hands of government security agents.[16]

---

15 Ibid., 59–61.
16 Mandela, *Part of My Soul*, 65, 71, 73, 77.

In the final analysis, apartheid was a system of oppression that undermined its Black victims by often turning them against each other. The dilemma faced by Black families is exemplified by the case of Caesarina Kona Makhoere's family; the parents were never there for the children because they had to do meager and humiliating jobs in order to ensure their basic survival. Like her own parents, she had to leave her child behind while serving six years in prison for fighting for the liberation of her people. The Makhoere family became even more dysfunctional as the system became even more relentless in its effort to rusticate each of the members. For instance, her father showed the security police Caesarina's place of hiding at a relative's home. Consequently, soon after the announcement of her five-year prison verdict by a white judge, Caesarina's father took ill and died.[17]

The sources used in this work include autobiographies, activist writings, scholarly writings, biographical writings, and government documents. In her autobiography *Part of My Soul Went with Him,* Winnie Mandela describes the experience of a Black woman married to a political activist during the apartheid period. She describes how her life became a public one because of her commitment to the struggle against apartheid. For example, her marriage ceremonies could not be completed because the government allowed Nelson very little time to leave Johannesburg for the village for his marriage with Winnie. She also describes how "life with him was like life without him" because he lived for his people and not just for his family. She describes her experience with the Treason Trial and the ordeals with Nelson's life sentence. Finally, she describes her life as a single parent who was constantly harassed, intimidated, arrested, detained or jailed, forcefully removed and relocated, and scrutinized by the agents of the apartheid government.

In another book, *Strikes Have Followed Me All My Life*, Emma Mashinini, a trade union activist, describes efforts to form a trade union that could be a voice for Black workers in South African industry. Before

---

17 Caesarina Kona Makhoere, *No Child's Play: In Prison Under Apartheid* (London: The Women's Press, Ltd, 1988), 12.

Emma's leadership, Black workers faced semi-slave working conditions. They had no basic human rights whatsoever. They could be hired and fired at any time. They were paid very low wages compared to their White counterparts. They had no employment benefits. Overall, Black industrial workers who made up about 70 percent of the total labor force during the apartheid era were treated like migrant workers in their own land. Emma describes the ordeals she went through with the police, the employers, and the prison system because she was a spokesperson on behalf of her people.[18]

In *No Child's Play: In Prison Under Apartheid*, Caesarina Kona Makhoere, a student activist involved in the Soweto uprising, describes her traumatic experience in the hands of apartheid security officers during her six years of incarceration. She discusses the trauma of fear and loneliness due to her separation from friends and relatives and denial of family support. She also discusses the pain caused to her by the knowledge of her father's ordeal in the hands of brutal security agents when he was forced by the latter to reveal her hiding place. Her trauma was exacerbated by the fact that subsequent to her arrest and long imprisonment, her father took ill and died under the weight of the guilt associated with his involuntary collaboration with those who oppressed his daughter.[19]

In *Cry Amandla: South African Women and the Question of Power*, June Goodman, an American journalist, comments on her interviews with Black and non-Black women of South Africa about their struggle against apartheid. She also comments on her interviews with key players in the apartheid regime, including security agents. Goodman's interviews reveal that while Black women generally spoke about the evils of apartheid and their determination to bring it down, White women were divided in their opinions on race relations in apartheid South Africa. Many, like Mrs. Gabrielle Malan, supported apartheid. While others, like Mary Benson, joined the struggle against the system.

---

18 Emma Mashinini, *Strikes Have Followed Me All My Life: A South African Autobiography* (New York: Routledge, 1991), xxx.
19 Makhoere, *No Child's Play*, 6.

It is noteworthy that, like Black women, White women who expressed opposition to apartheid received harsh treatment from the system. Like Black opponents of the regime, they were also labeled "Communists." In her interview with Goodman, Mary Benson describes the experience of being forced into exile by the apartheid regime:

> Exile is very, very painful. I often think South Africans have a peculiar anguish to their exile: something about the people left behind. Whenever I went back to South Africa, I felt the energy, joy, giftedness of the great mass of Black people that has been systematically kept down.[20]

Emma Mashinini, a trade union activist, writes about the poor and racist working conditions of Black workers under the apartheid regime. Black trade unions were illegal. Thus, they could not function freely like the White trade unions. Black unionists faced constant harassment, arrest, and detention without trial by the apartheid police. Black employees were paid very low wages and were often subjected to inhumane working conditions.[21] In spite of state-sponsored violence against them, industrial Black workers founded their own union in 1975, the Commercial, Catering, and Allied Workers' Union of South Africa (CCAWUSA). Female union leaders like Emma were constantly harassed, intimidated, arrested, interrogated or tortured, and charged with all kinds of violations. In fact, these women faced the possibility of being killed for acting as a voice for Black workers.

The combined effect of sexism, racism, and poverty forced many Black women to drop out of school during the apartheid era. Invariably, lack of education and specialized skills imposed further restrictions on their economic opportunities, as well as diminished their ability to fight the system. This is demonstrated by the case of Thenjie Mtintso, a bright student who nursed a desire to study medicine but was forced to

---

20 Goodwin, *Cry Amandla*, 155.
21 Mashinini, *Strikes Have Followed Me All My Life,* xxxi.

drop out of school because of her family's checkered financial situation. Unlike White students in a similar situation, Thenjie was unable to secure financial aid or a scholarship to pursue her dream.[22] Her situation can be understood in the context of the apartheid policy of using ethnic/racial classifications to ensure White control of power and resources. Not only did Pretoria's ethnic/racial classification scheme often fail to reflect a person's correct background, but it also was instrumental to the implementation of its policy of inequitable allocation of resources among members of different ethnic/racial groupings. Commenting on Thenjie's experience, Goodwin states,

> Like her mother, Thenjie is Xhosa. She was born in Soweto but declared by apartheid to be a "citizen" of Transkei, the first tribal homeland to be declared an independent country by South Africa and recognized only by South Africa.[23]

To consolidate White power under apartheid, the government enacted various discriminatory laws such as the Pass Laws and Stock Limitation, the Group Areas Act, the Voters' Representation Act, the Suppression of Communism Act, and the Bantu Authorities Act, to name a few.[24] On June 26, 1955, the African National Congress, in collaboration with Black women and other opposition groups, staged one of the biggest peaceful demonstrations in South Africa, during which the participants called on the government to repeal apartheid laws or face protests. As will be shown in the next chapters, the joint declaration by the above groups, the Freedom Charter, served as a legal and political framework for subsequent acts of resistance against White minority hegemony in South Africa.[25]

---

22 Goodwin, *Cry Amandla*, 13.
23 Ibid., 17.
24 Leo Kuper, *Passive Resistance in South Africa* (New Haven: Yale University Press, 1957), 248–249.
25 Mandela, *Part of My Soul*, 151–156. Thompson, Leonard, *A History of South Africa* (New Haven: Yale University Press, 1995), 208.

Notably, Black women were at the forefront of the struggle to translate the Freedom Charter into reality. Specifically, while they pursued the ultimate goal of dismantling apartheid, they demanded political and economic justice for Blacks and all South Africans. Some of their concerns were as follows: inhumane treatment of the Black labor force; urban and rural poverty among the Black families; Bantu education; passing laws imposed on Blacks in their native land; residential segregation and substandard infrastructure (or the lack thereof) in Black neighborhoods; arbitrary arrests and detention of Blacks; jail and imprisonment of Blacks without fair trials; frequent murder and disappearance of opponents of the apartheid regime; constant harassment and intimidation of Blacks by government security agents; the disenfranchisement of or denial of voting rights to Blacks; and classification of married Black women as minors, to mention but a few. This is of historical significance because boys became adults at about eighteen but women, no matter their age, were treated as minors (chapter 3).

This work is organized as follows: chapter 1 or the introduction presents an overview of the thesis. Chapter 2 deals with the status of Black women prior to apartheid, and the historical background of the apartheid regime. Chapter 3 discusses apartheid policies and their impacts on Black women. Chapter 4 highlights the special contributions and strategies of Black women to the struggle against apartheid and women's rights. It also emphasizes the importance of their effort to build a broad power base through the mechanism of political coalition with other groups. The concluding chapter reflects on the post-apartheid situation, with particular emphasis on the significance of South Africa's democratic constitution in relation to equity and fairness in the distribution of power and resources between Black women and other groups. The work of the Commission on Gender Equality will also be discussed in the conclusion.

CHAPTER 2

Black Women In Precolonial South Africa

Women were taught to keep away from the public discussions of men: they were to mind their work, and leave the *mahuku* (words) to men alone.[26]

—Margaret Kinsman

There is no doubt that many of the Bantu-speaking mixed farmers of Southern Africa attained a high level of material security and prosperity. In 1689, the Dutch commander of the Cape Colony interviewed the men who had survived the wreck of the *stavenisse* and spent nearly three years in Natal. He reported to Amsterdam that "the country is exceedingly fertile, and incredibly populous, and full of cattle, whence it is that lions and other ravenous animals are not apt to attack men, as they find enough tame cattle to devour." He added: "in their intercourse with each other they are very civil, polite, and talkative . . ." [27]

—Leonard Thompson

---

26 Margaret Kinsman, "Beasts of Burden: The Subordination of Southern Tswana Women, ca. 1800–1840," *Journal of Southern African Studies* v.10, n. 1 (October 1983): 48–49.
27 Leonard Thompson, *A History of South Africa* (New Haven: Yale University, 1995), 21.

Mmanthatisi is unusual in that she led her people herself during one of the greatest crises in Southern African History. Her husband, Mokotjo, had died in 1817, probably of illness, and she found herself faced with a succession struggle. Her eldest son, Sekonyela, was only about thirteen years old; he had not yet been circumcized and was not immediately eligible for the chieftaincy. Her brother-in-law, Sehalahala, seemed set to inherit, but Mmanthatisi was determined to prevent this and persuaded the elders of the group to accept her as regent.[28]

—David Sweetman

Introduction

PRECOLONIAL SOUTH AFRICA was inhabited by three indigenous groups, the Khoi, the San, and the Bantu; the first two groups are often referred to collectively as Khoisan because of their common ancestral origin. The San originally inhabited the southernmost tip of the Cape of South Africa. Organized in small bands, members of this small-sized people with yellow skin were noted for their good artistic skills and click language. Their subsistence was based on hunting and food gathering, thus necessitating frequent relocation to new areas in search of game, wild fruits, vegetables, and nuts. Because of their simple life, the San had few possessions. The men were responsible for hunting and for making decisions about relocation, while the women took care of the young and gathered food.

Coexisting with the San were the Khoi, who were herders and pastoralists. Although they had to move from one place to another in search of green pasture for their cattle and sheep, they generally

---

28 David Sweetman, *Women Leaders in African History* (Portsmouth, New Hampshire: Heinemann Educational Book Inc. 1984), 55.

maintained more stable settlements or communities than the San. Among the Khoi, economic and social status was determined by the number of cattle and sheep possessed by families. While the Khoisan shared similar myths, legends, and click languages, there were remarkable distinctions between the two groups in terms of physical stature and social organization. The Khoi were usually taller than the San and they lived in chiefdoms—a chiefdom consisting of several clans—with clan heads or chiefs as rulers of their respective communities. According to Leonard Thompson, a chiefdom was a "cluster of villages that recognized the authority of a single leader."[29] Unlike the San who lived in makeshift communities, the Khoi lived in political units (or chiefdoms), occupying a defined area under independent chiefs. These geopolitical entities were subdivided among subordinate chiefs, who acknowledged the authority of the superior chief. In 1809, for example, Hintsa, the Xhosa chief with 10,000 followers, had eleven subchiefs under him.[30]

The Bantu are the ancestors of the dark-skinned or "Black" South Africans, who originally inhabited the area north of the cape. Comprised of the Nguni-speaking people, the Sotho-Tswana, and the Xhosa, they formed the majority of the indigenous South African population. The primary economic activity of the Bantu groups consisted of mixed farming with some herding. Although they migrated when necessary, the Bantu lived in large kingdoms under the political leadership of powerful kings and enjoyed a far more stable lifestyle than the Khoisan. Like the Khoisan, Bantu culture was based on separate initiation rites for males and females, and gender-based division of labor in the family and the larger community.

The arrival of the Dutch in 1652 and the subsequent colonization of South Africa by the Europeans radically transformed the cultures of the indigenous groups as well as the course of their history. However,

---

29 Thompson, *History of South Africa*, 24; Monica Wilson, "The Nguni People," in Wilson and Thompson; *The Oxford History of South Africa* v. 1 (New York: Oxford University Press, 1969), 118–119; Leonard Thompson, "The Subjection of the African Chiefdoms, 1870–1898" in Wilson and Thompson, *The Oxford History*, v. 2, 245–247.
30 Monica Wilson, "The Nguni People," 117; Thompson, *History of South Africa*, 25.

many indigenous cultural practices managed to survive through to the present. This chapter explores the status of Black women in precolonial South Africa with the primary aim of examining the status of Black women in traditional society. Also examined are some of the changes brought about by the arrival of the Europeans and their impact on Black women. Finally, the implications of Britain's decision to hand over political power to White minority settlers in 1910—the formal installment of apartheid would wait until 1948—and the impacts of the Union Laws on Black women are examined.

Initiation Rites and Gender Roles in Precolonial Society

In precolonial South Africa, children were socialized along gender lines to play different roles in their families and the larger society. For example, boys were socialized into becoming good pastoralists, being in charge of the family's cattle, goats, and calves. This often required boys to stay away from the family from time to time since they had to guide the animals in the field. This gender training or socialization started as early as nine or ten years old.[31] Girls stayed at home helping their mothers with domestic work such as cooking, fetching water from the streams or springs, collecting wild plants, grinding grains, and farming. Overall, girls were raised to be hardworking and obedient to their fathers and later on their husbands, while boys were taught to raise livestock and be in control of their families.[32]

Puberty marked a critical phase in the lives of young people; it was the point at which boys and girls were required to make the transition to adulthood. Each community had an elaborate initiation ceremony or rite of passage to commemorate the end of childhood and to equip the initiates for their future roles in society as men and women. Boys and girls were required to spend a specified length of time at separate

---

31 Wilson, "The Nguni People," 47; Omer-Cooper, J. D. *History of Southern Africa* (Portsmouth, New Hampshire: Heinemann Educational Books, Inc. 1987), 15, 53–54; Thompson, *History of South Africa*, 22–25.
32 Wilson, "The Hunters and Herders," 48; Thompson, *History of South Africa*, 22–26.

initiation schools, where each group went through a meticulously designed process of final socialization or civic education, at the end of which they were considered adults. The initiation experience was different for girls and boys. The girls were required to spend only two months at the initiation school while for the boys the process took six months or three times as long as female initiation.[33]

The primary purpose of female initiation upon reaching puberty was to determine the girls' suitability for marriage and to prepare them for childbirth. A widow was designated to preside over female initiation or to act as a tutor. The tutor examined them internally, after which their hymens were pierced with a tuber. Girls were expected to be virgins at the time of initiation; if a girl had premarital sex, ostracism, and disgrace were some of the punishments. Subsequent to the examination process, they were given lessons on female sexuality. They were subjected to severe flogging during the process to prepare them for the pain of child labor.[34]

The girls also received lessons on the virtue of modesty, especially in regard to public affairs. They were instructed to "keep away from the public discussions of men: they were to mind their work, 'and leave the *mahuku* (words) to men alone.'"[35] It was made clear to the female initiates that severe penalties awaited a woman who did not adhere to the rule of silence. Her punishment included physical abuse. Girls were not expected to choose their future husbands—this was a parental responsibility. If a girl did not like her parents' choice, she was forced to accept it.[36] Girls were conditioned to a life of self-denial and subordination during the initiation process. They were made to live like "servants of the lowest caste" during the two-month period. They hewed wood, drew water, as well as performed other "feminine" tasks, and were also given some beating upon return.

---

33 Thompson, *History of South Africa*, 24–26.
34 Wilson, "The Nguni People," 49; Thompson, *History of South Africa*, 22–23.
35 Wilson, "The Hunters and Herders," 49; Thompson, *History of South Africa*, 22–26.
36 Wilson, "The Hunters and Herders," 48; Omer-Cooper, *History of Southern Africa*, 11.

The only time women were expected to be active in the community was during religious ceremonies. As Kinsman states,

The exception to the rule was religious activities, and it was here that much of women's sense of civic involvement and public concern may have been channeled. Religious ceremonies provided the major public forum for women's collective action: preparations for the rain-maker, sowing the chief's garden, dancing and singing in ceremonies intended to bring rain, all brought women together to express their involvement and concern in the community's well-being.[37]

The only public figures who were women were the oracles. The oracle was believed to have "seen God" and was warned about famine, war, or plenty.[38] Notably, women could only qualify for the role of oracles while men held the superior positions of rain-maker and priest. Although the oracles had some power in traditional society, the female occupants of this position were still highly marginalized as it was believed that spiritual power rested mainly with the rain-makers and the priests, who were men.

Girls emerged from the initiation ceremony mature women, ready to subordinate themselves to patriarchal control, work very hard for the good of the community, and to deny themselves basic economic, political, and social rights. At the end of the initiation ceremony, the girls were given a piece of hot iron that they held in their hands to demonstrate that their hands were ready for the challenges of womanhood.[39] They were ready for life under a social order in which they would not be permitted to accumulate personal wealth, play important roles in the public sphere, or chose their husbands. Interestingly, the initiation experience was also designed to prepare the women to minimize their expectations in regard to the men's contribution toward the upkeep of the family.[40]

---

37 Wilson, "The Hunters and Herders," 51.
38 Ibid., 51.
39 Ibid., 49; Thompson, *History of South Africa*, 22–23, 84.
40 Thompson, *History of South Africa*, 19, 22–27.

Traditional society did not prepare the men for domestic life. As a recompense, it gave the women the liberty to curse them out for being irresponsible. Accordingly, girls were allowed to conclude the humbling ceremony "with public expression of hostility towards men - for their laziness and their failure to labour for their families."[41] The initiation process for boys was designed to prepare them for vastly different roles in society. They were prepared for extra-domestic life and for leadership in the public sphere. According to Thompson,

> The educational system reinforced the hierarchical principle. At or soon after reaching puberty, boys were segregated from the rest of society for as long as six months and prepared for adult life. In the form that prevailed among the Basotho, a chief would convene a *lebollo* (initiation school) when one of his sons had reached the appropriate age. This was a dramatic episode in the life of a chiefdom.[42]

The chief had a responsibility to ensure that things went well during the male initiation period. He dramatized the historical importance of the August tradition through a public declaration, during which he impressed upon his community the pivotal responsibilities to be met by the male initiates as future leaders, farmers, and warriors. The chief was responsible for appointing a *mohlabani* (distinguished warrior), a *mesuoe* (instructors), and a *thipane* (surgeon), who performed very important aspects of the ceremony.[43] He was also responsible for selecting other adults who participated in the ceremony. Finally, he supplied the materials needed for the initiation—a bull, butterfat, and

---

41   Wilson, "The Hunters and Herders," 49; Thompson, *History of South Africa*, 19, 22–23.
42   Thompson, *History of South Africa*, 24; Mandela, *Long Walk to Freedom*, 25; Omer-Cooper, *History of Southern Africa*, 15, 53–54.
43   Thompson, *History of South Africa*, 24; Mandela, *Long Walk to Freedom*, 25–31; Omer-Cooper, *History of Southern Africa*, 15, 53–54.

most important of all, his personal *lenaka*.[44] The *lenaka* is "a horn, preferably a rhinoceros horn, containing a powder composed of a mixture of vegetable and animal materials and human flesh."[45] The butterfat was extracted from a bull or a cow captured by their enemies. The human flesh was cut from a killed enemy warrior. During the initiation process, the boys were subjected to different types of physical tests, including circumcision, and they received instructions on the customs and traditions of the community. During his time, Nelson Mandela was among twenty-six boys who participated in a circumcision ceremony arranged by the local chief. The boys were housed in two secluded huts (that is, a makeshift circumcision school) located on the bank of the Mbashe River. According to Mandela, women brought food to the boys from nearby villages, and during such occasions "we danced to their singing and clapping. As the music became faster and louder, our dance turned more frenzied and we forgot for a moment what lay ahead."[46]

The differences between girls' and boys' initiation ceremonies are noteworthy. In the first place, the girls were expected to provide themselves with everything they needed, including firewood and water, to prepare their food. In contrast, the boys' food was prepared at home and brought to the initiation school by their mothers throughout the six-month period. Further, in contrast to the girls, boys undergoing initiation were allowed to make special appearances as dancers at weddings and community festivals and were honored with gifts of cows, calves, and goats. They were taught special songs whose themes reflected the masculine values and taboos being instilled in them.[47] For example, male initiates from the Leribe district learned songs that emphasized that they did not eat fish. One of the songs, documented by David Livingstone, goes as follows: "I do not eat fish; A fish is a snake; A water

---

44 Thompson, *History of South Africa*, 24; Omer-Cooper, *History of Southern Africa*, 15.
45 Thompson, *History of South Africa*, 24.
46 Nelson Mandela, *Long Walk to Freedom*, 27.
47 Ibid., 25; Omer-Cooper, *History of Southern Africa*, 8; Thompson, *History of South Africa*, 24, 27, 84; July, *A History of the African People*, 112; Wilson, "The Sotho, Venda, and Tsonga" in Wilson and Thompson, *The Oxford History of South Africa* v. 1, 167.

snake; It makes me ill."[48] At the time, the Sotho and Nguni peoples distinguished themselves from the Khoikhoi and the San through the fish taboo. It was deemed unnecessary to teach the girls the same taboos as the boys since the former could technically lose their citizenship, as they often did when they married outside of the community.

As was noted earlier, the primary purpose of female initiation was to prepare the girls for marriage and domestic life. For the same reason, they were not entitled to the prestigious outing and musical performances that earned their male counterparts' spotlight and public adoration. Initiation ceremonies for boys were of historical significance; at the end of the process, they were received by the elders as adults and future leaders of the community, prepared to work closely with the young prince (and future chief) with whom they went through the initiation process. They were ready to take a wife and become fathers and heads of their own households. They are ready to become great farmers and herders. They were ready to go to war and to serve as orators, counselors, and elders. They were expected to conduct themselves as role models for the younger men in the community. The initiation experience instilled in the boys' self-confidence and a strong sense of belonging to the community by surrounding them with great support from the chief, their teachers, their families, and the entire community. Initiation was carefully orchestrated to transform boys into men and fathers, and girls into women and mothers.

Gender Relations in Precolonial Society

Precolonial South Africa was made up of autonomous societies in which social relations were governed by well-established norms, taboos, and laws, which won the admiration of early European visitors. For instance, following the wreck of the Dutch vessel *Stavenisse* in 1686, the Europeans were accommodated by the local communities. They

---

48 Wilson, "The Sotho, Venda, and Tsonga," 167; Thompson, *History of South Africa*, 24–28.

spoke highly of the hospitality and courtesy of the Xhosa people, their respect for their chiefs, and for the rule of law. The Europeans further observed that the indigenous peoples cared for kingship, seniority, and cattle. They noted the gaiety and humor of the women and the good manners of the men. They were impressed by the Xhosas' sophistication in poetry, oratory, dance, music, and song and other art forms.[49]

Wilson and Thompson further describe the social life of these native peoples in a more positive light. According to the authors, native South Africans were lively and full of pride in their customs: "In their intercourse with each other, they are very civil, polite and talkative, saluting each other, whether male or female, young or old, whenever they meet; asking whence they come, and whither they are going, what is their news, and whether they have learned any new dances or tunes . . ."[50] For example, the Nguni society had a lot of respect for their traditions, including traditional rituals. In fact, one of the duties of the chief was to "carry out the *amasiko,* the ritual . . ."[51] The chief was expected to keep the living and their ancestors connected through rituals.

Precolonial South African societies operated governmental systems under the leadership of chiefs. The position of Khoi chief was both hereditary and patriarchal; hence, women, including daughters of the royal family, participated in the political process only at the periphery. The chief was expected to marry many wives. He had the privilege to summon his people to work on his farm. He was the richest man in the community. Thompson describes the daily schedule and privileges of the chief as follows:

> A chief spent much of his time in the open-air meeting place near his personal hut. There, in cooperation with his counselors, who were drawn from the heads

---

49   Wilson, "The Nguni People" in Wilson and Thompson, *The Oxford History* v. 1, 128, 80–85, 233; Thompson, *History of South Africa*, 18, 21.
50   Wilson, "The Nguni People," 129.
51   Ibid., 118, 128; Omer-Cooper, *History of Southern Africa*, 12.

of homesteads, he regulated the affairs of his people, listening to complaints, settling disputes, and receiving visitors. He was the richest man in his territory. His subjects paid him sheep and cattle for settling their disputes, his men handed over to him any livestock they seized from neighboring chiefdoms, and he had the right to summon his people to work for him. They cultivated the fields of his senior wives, since he was expected to use their produce to entertain guests and feed the men when they were summoned to his village for political discussions or military purposes. A chief was thus rich enough to marry more wives and provide more generous hospitality than any of his subjects.[52]

European visitors noted that the Tswana and the Nguni had developed an efficient judicial system and a strong commitment to the rule of law. The *Kgotla,* which means both a courtyard and a court of law, was the center, physically and metaphorically, of every capital. European visitors found both the chief in *Dithakong* and the regent in *Kaditshwene* sitting in the *Kgotla* with counselors, settling disputes.[53] Some cases were minor, while murder, assault, witchcraft, and slander were considered very serious cases among the Tswana and Nguni. They were capital offenses against the chief. At both the village and the capital cities, the main thrust of the judicial process was to bring about reconciliation between the disputants and their families, with the possibility of imposing some penalty on the guilty party. When the local or village courts failed to resolve a given dispute, it was forwarded to the chief, who presided over the judicial system at the central government level.[54] Consistent with the pattern of socialization that culminated

---

52 Thompson, *History of South Africa*, 25; Omer-Cooper, *History of Southern Africa*, 12.
53 Wilson, "The Sotho, Venda, and Tsonga," 158; Mandela, *Long Walk to Freedom*, 20–22.
54 Wilson, "The Sotho, Venda, and Tsonga," 158; Thompson, *History of South Africa*, 2; Omer-Cooper, *History of Southern Africa*, 14–15.

in the initiation rites discussed earlier, the public sphere was generally regarded as the men's domain.

Khoi chiefdoms were made up of several clans, and although a chiefdom was linked to the constituent clans by ancestry, this relationship was flexible. This is because the Khoi were fiercely egalitarian and individualistic. In times of serious disagreement, the men would not hesitate to use the poison weapons—designed for hunting games—against each other or strangers. Sometimes, conflicts could lead to political fragmentation as some clans could decide to break away and find a new chiefdom.[55] Political decisions were made by adult males, who were usually summoned to the village gathering by the chief. They deliberated on a wide range of subjects, including war, farming, land rights, and the like.

In *History of South Africa*, J. D. Omer-Cooper documents aspects of public decision-making among the Khoisan people. According to the author,

> In many cases decisions were simply taken by discussion and agreement amongst the adult men. In some cases a leader was recognized as chief but his authority still depended on the agreement of the other adults. Each band occupied an extensive but clearly defined territory. Within this territory the band would migrate from waterhole to waterhole in pursuit of wild game and wild-growing vegetable foods. Movement across territorial boundaries into the area of another band required formal consent, and intrusion without permission was met by force.[56]

Gender inequality in the public sphere was reinforced by social and economic inequality between men and women in the family; while

---

55 Omer-Cooper, *History of Southern Africa*, 7, 13–14; Thompson, *A History of South Africa*, 29.
56 Omer-Cooper, *History of Southern Africa*, 3.

the women were expected to take care of the children and cook for the family, the men kept cattle, which was a major source of wealth and status in the society. As indicated earlier, the men were responsible for determining when the band would move and to where. They marked the boundaries separating other bands from their own, as well as making decisions on which outsiders should be admitted into their community. Similarly, when there was a need to use force to drive away an intruder, it was the adult men who carried out such a task.

The Bantu groups were organized in chiefdoms as well, and like the Khoisan, breakaway members of one chiefdom were welcomed into another. Like the Khoisan, the Bantu were culturally diverse; some of the constituent groups include the Venda, Kalaka, Xhosa, Sotho, Tswana, Ovambo, Ndebele, and Zizi.[57] Given the strong patrilineal/polygamous system, gender relations among the Bantu were heavily skewed in favor of the men, who controlled both political and economic power in the family and the larger society. Wealthy men and community leaders often married several wives. Each wife and her children lived in separate homes and cultivated their own land. The first son of the most senior wife succeeded his father. The men kept cattle, and the more cattle a man had the more wives he could have since bridewealth (*lobola*) was often paid with cattle.[58]

Perhaps gender inequality in Bantu society was most acute among the Tswana where the women were treated like third-class citizens. In the Tswana social structure, adult men (sometimes referred to as elders) came before the sons (who were to inherit political, economic, and social powers from their fathers). The women occupied the bottom of the social hierarchy and were expected to respect every male member of the community. Tswana law excluded women from getting involved in public affairs. Consequently, they were not allowed to participate in legal proceedings. On the other hand, the men served as the chief's counselors; such individuals helped the chief in settling a variety of cases, which included theft, adultery, and minor quarrels among rival

---

[57] Ibid., 10–11.
[58] Ibid., 11, 13, 89; Thompson, *History of South Africa*, 23.

wives, to mention but a few. Since the women were not allowed to have a voice in the public arena, they had to be represented by a male relative even when they were directly involved in a court case.[59]

According to Margaret Kinsman,

> Tswana women were caught in a state of legal minority in the early nineteenth century: they depended on men for representing them in court cases and in all legal transactions; they were physically excluded from participation in public political debates; they were expected to act in strict obedience to their husbands and elders; and they were subject to violent reprimands and social chastisement if acting otherwise. Although the legal position of Tswana women has been mitigated since then, they remain as a group subordinated.[60]

Women who did not play by the rules were subject to severe penalties, which often included corporal punishment. Concurring with the above views, Hoyt Alverson stated that "generally men dominate women psychologically. . . . The relations between the sexes are seen as based on a proper inequality."[61]

As the saying goes, there is an exception to every rule, and precolonial South Africa certainly had its own exceptions when it came to gender relations. Notably, the presence of prominent female leaders in precolonial South Africa and elsewhere meant that Black women were capable of leadership in the public sphere wherever they had the

---

59   Kinsman, "Beasts of Burden," 39.
60   Ibid., 39. Thompson, *History of South Africa*, 19; Omer-Cooper, *History of Southern Africa*, 11.
61   Hoyt Alverson in Kinsman, "Beasts of Burden," 39; Thompson, *History of South Africa*, 22–23, 25–27; 29; June Goodwin, *Cry Amandla! South African Women and the Question of Power* (New York: Africana Publishing Company, 1984), 188; Helene Perold, *Working Women: A Portrait of South Africa's Black Women Workers* (Johannesburg: Ravan Press Pty. Ltd, 1985), 121–122.

opportunity. This was also true, as we will see later, of Black women in the anti-apartheid resistance.

A frequently cited historical example is that of Queen Mmanthatisi of the Sotho kingdom, who succeeded her late husband to the throne. Married to Mkokojo of Tlokwa Sotho, Mmanthatisi became the chief's "great wife" in view of her royal background. She bore two future chiefs, Sekongela and Mota, as well as her only daughter, Ntitse. However, when her husband died in 1817, the kingdom of Sotho faced a succession crisis because thirteen-year-old Sekonyela was still uncircumcised and too young to take over his father's throne. To prevent her brother-in-law, Sehalahala, from inheriting the throne, Mmanthatisi convinced the elders to accept her as regent so that she could rule the kingdom until her first son was of age. She proved herself to be an effective leader throughout her reign. Among other things, she effectively handled some serious border conflicts, and during the Mfecane, she was able to hold her people together with the help of a strong standing army. When Mpangazita and his army invaded Sotho around 1822, he "did not expect a woman to resist in the way Mmanthatisi did."[62]

Notably, not all analysts agree that precolonial South Africa was very tolerant of gender inequality. For instance, S. M. Molema, a South African scholar who studied Southern Tswana society, recognized that there were serious problems with gender relations in that society. However, he tried to justify the problem by highlighting what he saw as the "benefits" of the patriarchal system, such as the "openness of material giving and the continued supports of the extended family—which were offered to women in the place of equality."[63] Molema's statement about material support to women is related to such once-in-a-lifetime gestures as the gift of two to three cows that fathers gave to their daughters at marriage. Unfortunately, this pales to insignificance compared to lands that male children inherited from their fathers in a patriarchal system. More to the point, the gift of cows to women in Tswana society was

---

62 Sweetman, *Women Leaders in African History*, 57; Omer-Cooper, *History of Southern Africa*, 61.
63 Kinsman, "Beasts of Burden," 39; Omer-Cooper, *History of Southern Africa*, 61.

more symbolic than substantive since the men took care of cattle. In other words, the woman's husband automatically inherited the cows. Interestingly, Molema seems to suggest that men do not receive or need any support from extended family.[64] Like other men who try very hard to rationalize patriarchy, Molema appears to argue that women should be grateful to the patriarchal system that deprived them of their basic political and economic rights.

Conclusion

The preceding discussion dealt with the role of women in precolonial South Africa. Despite their hard work in the economic arena, Black women generally occupied an inferior position in precolonial society. Although they made critical contributions toward the upkeep of the family and the larger community, they were generally excluded from political, economic, and social activities that had a major impact on the distribution of power and resources among members of the community. Indeed, women were regarded as the subordinates of men within and outside the family. During their initiation, girls were instructed that women should leave the political activity to men as they were not supposed to be heard. Male relatives were expected to speak on their behalf at public forums such as at the chiefs' courts. Women were not recognized as orators, warriors, or community leaders. It was believed that they did not possess leadership abilities. In short, women were raised to have children and to take care of the house while boys were raised to act as leaders in the family and community.

As will be discussed in the next chapter, South Africa underwent radical transformation following the arrival of the Europeans in the seventeenth century. After the takeover of their lands and cattle by the Europeans, the natives had to endure slave-like conditions in their homelands, forced to work for the European settlers. The political, social, and economic status of Black women worsened progressively

---

64 Kinsman, "Beasts of Burden," 42–43; Omer-Cooper, *History of Southern Africa*, 13.

in the "new" South Africa as political and economic control changed hands from the early Dutch settlers to the British, and then from British colonialists back to a White minority settler regime. Not only were Black men and women subordinated to the Europeans on the basis of the presumed racial superiority of the latter; in addition, Black women were victimized on the basis of class and gender distinctions.

CHAPTER 3

Black Women And Apartheid Laws

Then there is the famous passage, quoted by Lenin, in which Rhodes recounted how he attended a meeting of the unemployed in the East End in 1895 and "listened to the wild speeches, which were just a cry for 'bread,' 'bread,' 'bread,'" and became convinced that the only alternative to civil war was that "we colonial statesmen must acquire new lands to settle the surplus population, to provide new markets for the goods produced in the factories and mines." However wild some of his dreams, the empire remained for Rhodes essentially "a bread and butter question."[65]

—Joseph Lenin reporting on Cecil Rhodes

I remember most of all how they cursed us when we couldn't keep up. I was in a department headed first by an Afrikaner called Mrs. Smith and then by a German-speaking man, Mr. Becker. He used to shout and scream at us, sometimes for no reason at all, and it wasn't unusual for ten people to be dismissed a day. They were always saying you have to push. They would say, "*Roer jou gat*," which means, "Push your arse" – "Come on,

---

[65] M. E. Chamberlain, *The Scramble for Africa* (London: Longman Group Limited, 1974), 76.

push your arse and be productive." . . . at the back of your mind you were concerned about the welfare of your children. You would be torn in two, because you were at work and in your mind you were at home. This is the problem of the working mother: you are divided. You are only working because you have to.[66]

—Emma Mashinini

As an occupational group, the almost 800,000 black women who are domestic workers in contemporary South Africa show a considerable variety of characteristics. Some are part of an urban industrial proletariat; others are migrant workers who send money to a family living in the homelands or on a white-owned farm. However, the prevailing characteristic of the domestic worker's situation in South Africa is exploitation. They are "trapped" within a tightly woven structure of constraints: a condition of subjugation and immobility.[67]

—Jacklyn Cock

Introduction

THIS CHAPTER WILL discuss the historical background of apartheid, apartheid laws, and their implications for Black women under the subtopics Black women and White domination before apartheid, and Black women and apartheid laws. Essentially, the chapter focuses on laws and practices that had a major impact on various

---

66 Emma Mashinini, *Strikes Have Followed Me All My Life: A South African Autobiography* (New York: Routledge, Chapman and Hall, Inc.1991), 14.
67 Jacklyn Cock, *Maids and Madams: A Study in the Politics of Exploitation* (Johannesburg: Ravan Press, 1980), 7.

aspects of the lives of Black women and their family members: land tenure, housing, employment, political association, population control, franchise, education, health, local administration, human rights, to mention but a few.

By the late fifteenth century, Africans living in the area that would later become South Africa had developed a vibrant culture. However, the coming of the Europeans, especially the Dutch, radically changed the course of their history. The Europeans made first contact with South Africa as early as 1487 when a Portuguese expedition led by Bartholomew Dias reached Mossel Bay or the Cape of Good Hope. Subsequent visits by different European groups took place between 1487 and 1652.[68] Monica Wilson indicates that during the above period the natives accommodated European survivors of shipwrecks, who decided to settle among them, with some marrying South African women. According to the author, "the survivors of the *Belem* met a man who had been left behind by the 1593 party as a boy, with the Chief Luspance, because he was too ill to travel. He 'was now very rich and had three wives and many children.'"[69] Although relations between Africans and Europeans were generally cordial before the middle of the seventh century, the action of the Belem survivors carried ominous implications relative to future conflicts between the two groups. After Chief Luspance and his people had helped the group purchase calves and cattle that they needed to start a new life in the area, the Europeans turned around and shot their African hosts.[70]

Unlike Western and Eastern Africa, Southern Africa presented a little problem to European visitors. The convergence of favorable factors facilitated European penetration of the hinterland; not only was the climate temperate, but the region was very sparsely populated by wandering groups of so-called Bushmen and Hottentots, people

---

68 Leonard Thompson, *A History of South Africa* (New Haven: Yale University Press, 1995), 21.
69 Monica Wilson, "The Nguni People" in Wilson and Thompson, *The Oxford History of South Africa* (New York: Oxford University Press, 1969), v.1, 83.
70 Ibid., 83.

currently called the San and Khoikhoi. Yet the southernmost tip of Africa attracted little attention from the Portuguese, who preferred to call at East African ports like Mozambique on their way to South Asia. When the Dutch decided to establish a base at Table Bay in 1652, the facility "was intended only as a service station for ships of the Dutch East India Company going to and from the East, but a few company employees remained at the Cape after their discharge and began to farm."[71] As indicated by their own accounts, the Europeans had very positive impressions of their South African hosts during the early stages of their contact with the latter. According to Wilson, a European journalist reported that

> the men of this country are very lean and upright, tall of stature, and handsome. They can endure great labour, hunger, and cold . . . They are so light that they can run over the rugged mountains as fleetly as stags. They are clothed in skins which hang over their shoulders to the knees; these are cow-hides, but they have the art of dressing them until they are as soft as velvet.[72]

Soon after their arrival at the Cape of Good Hope, the Dutch immigrants (later known as the Boers or Afrikaners) began to expand into the hinterland. Notably, South Africa derived its multiracial character and concomitant social conflicts from what would become a drawn-out process of European domination. During the period 1652 through 1795, when there was a steady migration of the Dutch to South Africa, the former embarked on an aggressive expansionist policy. To satisfy their need for a cheap labor supply, they conquered and forced the Khoikhoi and the San to work on their farms. If they had to continue to resist European domination they risked systematic extermination; thus, these native peoples had no other choice but to serve the invaders.

---

71 Chamberlain, *The Scramble for Africa*, 14.
72 Wilson, "The Nguni People" in Wilson and Thompson, *The Oxford History of South Africa*, v.1, 82.

During the period, the Dutch also imported slave labor from Indonesia, India, Ceylon, Madagascar, and Mozambique.[73] The sexual exploitation of both African women and Asian women by European men produced the "Colored" community in South Africa (now called Mixed Race).[74]

Among the prominent groups that emerged from the native communities, especially the Nguni, were the Zulu in the north and the Xhosa in the South. These two groups—as well as the Sotho in the South, the Pedi in the east, and the Tswana in the West—practiced mixed farming and spoke different dialects of the Bantu language.[75] The Xhosa were good cattle and sheep herders, and cattle was the most valuable commodity in their economy. The male members of the family took good care of the cattle. According to Ludwig Alberti, an employee of the Dutch government as commandant of the garrison at Fort Frederick (later Port Elizabeth) in 1803 through 1806, the Xhosa

> live principally by cattle-breeding. For the well-being of the family, a sufficient number of cattle are required, whose attendance and treatment is the sole responsibility of the father of the family, in which he is assisted by his sons. The Kaffir's cattle is the foremost and practically the only subject of his care and occupation, in the possession of which he finds complete happiness . . . he also attends to the milking of the cows and generally to everything requiring attention in cattle raising.[76]

The men were also good hunters. Xhosa women planted sorghum, millets, pumpkins, watermelons, calabashes, and beans and yams in some places.[77] They practiced an extended family system and took good care of the sick and the old. It was a male-dominated society

---

73   M. F. Katzen, "White Settlers and the Origin of a New Society, 1652–1778," in Wilson and Thompson, *The Oxford History of South Africa*, v. 1, 183–184.
74   Thompson, *A History of South Africa*, 66.
75   Ibid., 16.
76   Ibid., 18.
77   Ibid., 19.

in which the man controlled both the agricultural produce and the cattle wealth.[78] Alberti also noted that the Xhosa were not a warlike people, instead they wanted a stable community for raising their cattle.[79] The Xhosa kingdom was ruled by the Tshawe royal family, and new members were easily welcomed into the kingdom with all the rights, privileges, and responsibilities as long as they accepted the authority of the Tshawe.[80]

Although South Africa's early immigrant community was deeply divided, the constituent groups always maintained a unified front in their dealings with the local population. In the late eighteenth century, the Europeans reached the understanding that

> the government of the Cape could no longer be conducted on the assumption that it was essentially a refreshment station: the problems of a multi-racial colonial society had become too pressing to be ignored. The turning point came in the 1770s because the frontiersmen could no longer cope alone with war against San and Xhosa simultaneously. Government intervention became necessary.[81]

But the so-called Dutch Batavian Republic was barely holding on when Great Britain took over the Cape colony in 1795.[82] Like other European powers, the British harbored colonial ambitions in Africa, and they wanted to prevent France from taking over the Cape since the Netherlands was a weak power. Furthermore, Britain regarded the Cape peninsula as a stepping stone to South Asia, where the English East India Company was conducting a highly profitable trade.[83]

---

78 Ibid., 22–23.
79 Ibid., 27.
80 Ibid., 27–30.
81 Ibid., 183.
82 Thompson, *A History of South Africa*, 52, 73.
83 Wilson, "The Nguni People" in Wilson and Thompson, *The Oxford History*, 52–53.

With the imposition of British rule, the Afrikaners faced two mortal foes: the indigenous peoples of South Africa and the British. The 1814 Anglo-Dutch peace settlement showed that European colonizers were cognizant of the need for a collaborative response to local resistance in spite of an obvious conflict of interest among themselves.[84] Furthermore, between 1811 and 1812, the British and the Dutch joined forces to expel Africans from the territory west of the Fish River. Apart from the strategic advantage of coordinating their forces, the European invaders had superior weapons. Also, they took advantage of traditional rivalries that undermined solidarity among the African communities.[85]

This first act of expulsion of Africans from their homeland was a precedent for the pass laws and similar measures designed to promote White racist domination in colonial South Africa.[86] From that point on, Africans were only allowed in their former homelands as tenants and migrant laborers. Specifically, Black women who lost their homes and farmlands were forced to work as tenants and maids for European households in return for meager incomes. Although the pass laws were repealed in 1828, they would be reinstated after British rule by White minority administrations.[87]

Unfortunately, African groups continued to be at war with each other even though they faced the danger of possible extinction in the face of formidable enemies. For example, political crises resulting from the hegemonic ambitions of King Shaka Zulu helped make European conquest possible. From 1816 through 1828, this powerful African king embarked on an aggressive policy of territorial expansion that led to the creation of the Zulu kingdom. Under Shaka's autocratic leadership, Africans located southeast of the area were engaged in constant warfare, the Zulu *Mfecane* or "the time of trouble."[88] In 1828, Shaka was killed by two of his half-brothers and his personal servant while his soldiers

---

84 Ibid., 52.
85 Thompson, *A History of South Africa*, 73.
86 Ibid., 73–75.
87 Ibid., 304, 310.
88 Ibid., 231.

were away on an expedition, and the resulting power vacuum made his Zulu people more vulnerable to European domination.⁸⁹ The defeat of the Zulu army at Ulundi by the combined armies of the Afrikaners and British in 1879 left an enduring impact on Shaka's kingdom, which went into extinction before the end of the century (notably, earlier on in January 1879, the Europeans were defeated by the Zulu army at the battle of Isandhlwana).⁹⁰

Anglo-Afrikaner collaboration against the indigenous people masked the growing rift between the two groups. Between 1835 and 1840, a group of Afrikaners (or the *Voortrekkers*) numbering about five thousand took their Colored servants with them and left the Cape colony in search of a new settlement free of British interference.⁹¹ Between 1850 and 1854, they established the Transvaal and Orange Free States, which led to the further displacement and dislocation of the indigenous populations. Meanwhile, the British took over Natal in 1843. In 1867, diamond mining started in Griqualand West. The following year, Britain annexed Lesotho, also known as Basutoland. The two European groups continued their war of nerves over control of natural and human resources in South Africa.⁹² Colonial greed and concomitant conflict of interest between the British and the Afrikaners resulted in the famous South African War of 1899–1902, through which the British established their hegemony in South Africa.⁹³ The Africans, who had feared Britain's betrayal and had suffered as much as everyone else during the war, were actually betrayed by the British as it became evident that their interests did not matter.⁹⁴

In 1906 and 1907, the British government embarked on a discriminatory policy through which Europeans in the four colonies

---

89 Ibid., 85.
90 J. D. Omer-Cooper, *History of Southern Africa* (London: James Currey Ltd. 1987), 114–116; Thompson, *A History of South Africa*, 114–127.
91 Omer-Cooper, *History of Southern Africa*, 35, 70–81.
92 Ibid., 117.
93 Thompson, *A History of South Africa*, 141.
94 Ibid., 153; Leo Kuper, "African Nationalism in South Africa" in Wilson and Thompson, *The Oxford History of South Africa*, v. 2, 439–442.

(the Cape, Natal, the Transvaal, and the Orange Free State) were placed under parliamentary governments, while Africans and Asians were excluded from all forms of political participation.[95] As if this was not enough, in 1910, the British joined the republics to form the Union of South Africa.[96] Ultimately, the decision by British authorities to transfer political control of independent South Africa to the minority European population in 1910 would clear the ground for the emergence of apartheid. Following Britain's withdrawal, the Afrikaners moved swiftly to consolidate their economic and political power. In 1912, the Africans began to register their protest against these developments by founding the South African Native National Congress (NNC), later renamed the African National Congress (ANC).[97]

The period between 1913 and the late 1930s witnessed some important developments in South African history. For example, in 1913, the Natives Land Act was enacted, which limited Africans' land ownership or leases to the reserves. This period witnessed the beginning of a number of segregation laws as well. Between 1914 and 1919, South Africa, as a member of the British Empire, fought in World War I on the Allied side. In 1917, the Anglo American Corporation was founded, and in 1921, the South African Communist party was founded. In 1936, the Natives Representation Act was passed, and African parliamentary voters were placed on a separate roll. By implication, the political rights of Africans in the Cape province were weakened as Africans who qualified to vote could only elect Whites to represent them in parliament.[98] At the same time, the structure of the South African economy was becoming favorable to the White minority population as Blacks were increasingly being pushed to the margins. According to Thompson:

> The material expectations of the founders of the Union of South Africa were fulfilled. Between 1910 and 1948,

---

95 Ibid., 144, 149.
96 Ibid., 152–153; Robert W. July, *A History of the African People* (Prospect Heights, Illinois: Waveland Press, Inc. 1998), 345–347.
97 Thompson, *A History of South Africa*, 156.
98 Ibid., 157–170.

the economy weathered the Great Depression, and the national income of the country increased more than three times in real terms. The gold-mining industry made a major contribution to the national budget and provided enough foreign exchange for essential imports, especially heavy machinery and fuel oil.[99]

As they filled the power vacuum left by the British, the Afrikaner community experienced radical transformation as many Whites were able to move up the socioeconomic ladder.[100] In other words, British colonialism was replaced by a neocolonial system that continued to preserve European hegemony in South Africa at the expense of Africans and other non-European groups.

During the years following the end of World War I, elements of the Afrikaner elites formed "the Broederbond, a quasi-secret society of deeply nationalistic persuasion . . . for the establishment of an Afrikaner-controlled nation."[101] Important founding members of this organization included Jan Smuts, D. F. Malan, Louis Botha, and J. B. M. Hertzog.[102] Not only did the founding of the Broederbond (or brotherhood) mark the beginning of a modern Afrikaner nationalist movement in South Africa, these leaders claimed that it was designed to emancipate their people from poverty, provide educational opportunities for their children, and promote Afrikaner language and culture. Ultimately, the Broederbond was intended as an institutional and ideological mechanism to ensure Afrikaner dominance in the economic, political, and social spheres of modern South Africa. Robert July describes later Broederbond leader Dr. Hendrick Verwoerd "as a leading Afrikaner intellectual and advocate of white supremacy" who translated the racist theory of the organization into a blueprint for action.[103]

---

99 Ibid., 154.
100 Omer-Cooper, *History of Southern Africa*, 171.
101 July, *A History of African People*, 452.
102 Omer-Cooper, *History of Southern Africa*, 173.
103 July, *A History of African People*, 444.

While Botha and Smuts wanted to work with the English-speaking Europeans, Malan and Hertzog preferred to promote and protect only the interests of the Afrikaners. In their view, South Africa should emancipate itself from British imperialism. While Botha and Smuts would carry out Britain's requests during World War I, their opponents saw the war years as an opportunity to revolt against Britain and secure full autonomy. After Botha's death in 1919, he was succeeded by Smuts, who continued with their policy of reconciliation, and this continued to make their faction unpopular among the Afrikaners. In 1924, Smuts lost the election to Hertzog, who seized the opportunity to consolidate Afrikaner power. Between 1924 and 1933, Hertzog introduced some new legislation in favor of the Afrikaners. Capital was made available to White farmers, and prices for farm produce were guaranteed. Further, the government supported the steel manufacturing industry and protected White workers at the expense of Blacks. Afrikaans and English were made the official languages of South Africa. Most importantly, White women were enfranchised while Black women continued without voting rights.[104]

In March 1933, Hertzog and Smuts formed a coalition government, with Hertzog as prime minister and Smuts as deputy prime minister. In this year's elections, the coalition won 144 of the 154 seats in Parliament, and at the end of the year, the two groups formed the United Party. On the other hand, disgruntled English-speaking Europeans in Natal formed the Dominion Party. Dr. D. F. Malan left Hertzog's group and formed the Purified National Party.[105] Following the enactment of the Statute of Westminster in 1931 and the Status of the Union Act in 1934, South Africa became a sovereign state.[106] The historical implications of this development were enormous. First, legislation passed by the

---

104 Thompson, *A History of South Africa*, 157–160.
105 Omer-Cooper, *History of Southern Africa*, 176–7, 183, 194.
106 Ibid., 173, 200; Thompson, "The Compromise of Union" in Wilson and Thompson, *The Oxford History of South Africa*, v. 2, 363; Rene De Villiers, "Afrikaner Nationalism" in Wilson and Thompson, v. 2, 392–393; Leo Kuper, "African Nationalism in South Africa" in Wilson and Thompson, v. 2, 439–441; Jack Spence, "South Africa and the Modern World" in Wilson and Thompson, v. 2, 484–485, 495–501.

South African Parliament was no longer subject to external scrutiny by the British Parliament, even when such actions discriminated against certain groups. Second, individuals and groups who had concerns about the actions of the Pretoria regime could not go to London with their complaints. Finally, South Africa's sovereign status put the Afrikaners in the position to promote their interests aggressively, to the detriment of non-White groups.

The Natives Representation Act was enacted in 1936. This law mandated Africans in the Cape to elect three Whites to represent them in the House of Assembly, and four Whites to represent them in the senate. At the same time, the Natives Representative Council was established to act as an advisory body on behalf of Blacks.[107] Notably, the United Party began to decline by 1939 when Smuts and Hertzog disagreed over South Africa's World War II policy. While Hertzog stood for neutrality, Smuts favored joining Britain in the war. Smuts argued for votes to be taken in the Parliament, and the result was 80 to 67 in favor of joining the Allied powers. Against this backdrop, Hertzog's request for the Parliament to be dissolved for another election was denied by the governor-general. He resigned, and Smuts succeeded him as prime minister.[108]

Meanwhile, the Dominion Party was a local party in Natal, while the Purified National Party, with its doctrine of White supremacy supported by the Broederbond, was a national party that appealed to Afrikaner nationalism and interests. Notably, at this time the Afrikaner population was benefitting from state mandated-compulsory education for Whites, urbanization, and an improved standard of living.[109] Malan and his followers took advantage of the quarrels between Hertzog and Smuts as Hertzog's followers joined their party, which worked hard to "fulfill a divinely ordained role in the continent."[110] The Afrikaners or *Volk* people compared their life in South Africa with that of the Israelites

---

107 Thompson, *A History of South Africa*, 161.
108 Ibid., 162.
109 Ibid., 162; Omer-Cooper, *History of Southern Africa*, 176.
110 Omer-Cooper, *History of Southern Africa*, 176–178.

in Egypt and claimed to be guided by a divine destiny. They founded the Day of the Covenant, an annual celebration of Afrikaner nationalism that also commemorated their defeat of the Zulu at the battle of Blood River.[111] In 1938, "the centenary of the *voortrekkers'* victory over the Zulu offered the perfect opportunity for the Broederbond to launch its new strategy."[112] In the 1940s, Malan and his group continued to consolidate their political power by promoting Afrikaner culture, history, and nationalism and would reap its benefits in the general elections of 1948, which swept the Purified National Party into power.

Black South Africans virtually lost control over their political and economic future. Dispossessed of their lands, cattle, and resources, most of them would have to rely on selling their labor to White households and White-owned businesses to scratch out meager incomes. They lost their freedom of expression, association, and movement. As the men worked in the cities as migrant laborers, African mothers had to almost abandon their own families and children to work for European women as domestic servants and nannies.[113] For Black women, the situation was even more serious. With the men increasingly spending long periods of time away from their families in order to provide cheap labor for Whites as migrant workers, the women carried the responsibilities of keeping their families together. In their effort to combine work in and outside the family, these women were subjected to the triple discriminations of race, class, and gender in White-controlled South Africa.

Black Women and White Domination Before Apartheid

The legal status assigned by the White minority regime to different individuals and groups in South Africa carried specific social, political, and economic implications. Black women were defined as legal minors; thus, by law, they were subsumed under their husbands and male

---

111 Ibid.
112 Ibid., 177.
113 Caesarina Kona Makhoere, *No Child's Play: In prison under apartheid* (The Women's Press Ltd., London, 1988), 2.

relatives, who alone could deal directly with the system.[114] This scheme was aimed at undermining the Black community in view of the fact that apart from giving legal approval to gender-based prejudice and discrimination against Black women, the government subordinated Black men and women alike on the basis of race and class. While this divide-and-rule strategy was intended to maximize power for the White minority in South Africa, it raised the stakes very high for Black, women who had to deal with the triple handicap of race, class, and gender.

As will be shown in this section, the legal foundation for apartheid was set up long before 1948, when racial separation was formally adopted in South Africa. The British abolished slaveholding in their empire in 1833; however, in 1841, the government established the Masters and Servants Ordinance, and in 1856, the Masters and Servants Act.[115] These two laws were aimed at giving White farmers absolute authority over the lives of Black laborers and their families. These laws made it mandatory for Black laborers to adhere to unfair terms of contracts that were determined by White landlords. Failure to do so automatically earned the offending individuals unusually harsh punishments, which included flogging and/or eviction. The relationship between Blacks and their White employers was master-slave like, and Blacks were expected to carry out instructions without question or be treated like criminals. The system of justice allowed White landlords to take the law into their own hands.[116] As a result, the majority of disputes between Blacks and Whites did not get to the courts since the judicial system invariably backed the latter. Commenting on disputes between Black laborers and White employers, Waldman states that

---

114 Jashodhara Tripathy, "Plight of Black Women in South Africa: Feminism Reinforced Sans Humanism," *Africa Quarterly* v. 14, n. 1–3 (1985): 57–60; Sean Redding, "Legal Minors and Social Children: Rural African Women and Taxation in the Transkei, South Africa," *African Studies Review* v. 36, n. 3 (December 1993): 49–68; Fatima Meer, "Women in the Apartheid Society," in *United Nations Centre Against Apartheid: Notes and Documents* (April 1985): 5–10.
115 Linda Waldman, "Monkey in a Spiderweb: the Dynamics of Farmer Control and Paternalism," *African Studies* v. 55, n.1 (1996): 68.
116 Ibid., 68.

rarely did these "breaches of the law" find their way to court and when they did . . . the ruling was almost always in the "master's" favour. Mostly, however, the matter was settled beyond the bounds of the court, on the farm, with the farmer determining the punishment. This ranged from flogging with the *sjambok* (hide whip), which was a normal and common feature of farm service, to the eventual eviction of the "offender" and his/her dependents from the farm.[117]

Notably, White landlords and their relatives made no distinctions between Black men and women when it came to mistreating them. Black adults were called derogatory names such as *meid* (maid) or *kaffirmeid* (kaffir maid) for women, *meisie* for (girls), and *mannetjie* (little man) for men.[118] As if all these were not enough, White farmers insisted on exercising control over the personal lives of Black parents as well as those of their children. Black women (and men) watched helplessly while their children were beaten by White masters and their relatives. They were not in a position to raise questions when, as was often the case, their White employers decided to stop their children from attending school.[119] White landlords could abuse Black children under the guise of instilling "moral values" in them. Since women traditionally played a dominant part in the upbringing of children in African societies, these acts of socialization by White landlords and their relatives became subtle indictments of their failure as mothers.[120]

Similarly, White landlords and their wives often made critical personal choices pertaining to sexuality on behalf of Black women; in many cases, they forced Black women to be sterilized to avoid the "responsibility" of raising a large number of children. Waldman notes that during her field research on a White-owned farm, "Mrs. van Wyk

---

117 Ibid., 68.
118 Ibid., 68–78.
119 Ibid., 66.
120 Ibid., 70, 78.

wanted Meid to be sterilised so that she could not have any more children."¹²¹ Obviously, the hidden agenda behind the paternalistic behavior of these White farmers was simple. Although they needed cheap Black labor to work their farms, like the rest of the White community, they viewed the growth of the Black population as a serious threat to White power. Further, White farmers wanted Black employees to have small families so the parents could concentrate on being good (productive) laborers. Waldman also observed that Black women lost total control over their children's lives as well because "whenever an adolescent girl fell pregnant, her mother was the last to know."¹²² This was because both Black women and their children were treated with little or no respect by the White farmers, and as a result, these women lost their parental duties and control.

The hut tax, which was first imposed on Africans in 1878, was used to reinforce the traditional, though bogus, the notion that men were the legal heads of Black households.¹²³ Among the Xhosa, the hut tax was nicknamed *irafu* or "smiling tax" because African men paid this tax for the first time with smiles. This was not because they liked paying money to the state without representation, but because the state had finally recognized their passage into adulthood (the colonial system and Christian missionaries disapproved of the traditional initiation ceremony that ushered young men into adulthood).¹²⁴ Ironically, while the sons of Black women were recognized as adults by the state, their mothers and sisters were legally their subordinates. Black women could have access to land only through their husbands or male relatives.¹²⁵ Yet Black women played a dominant role relative to the survival of their families. They took care of their families, farmed the land, built new huts, or repaired old ones. Notably, in certain cases they paid taxes

---

121 Ibid., 80–82.
122 Ibid., 81.
123 Sean Redding, "Legal Minors and Social Children: Rural African Women and Taxation in the Transkei, South Africa," *African Studies Review* v. 36, n. 3 (December 1993): 50.
124 Ibid., 58–59.
125 Ibid., 51, 60.

on behalf of their absent husbands who were away on migrant labor contracts. The women had to pay taxes for their men because delinquent tax payments brought punishment on the entire family; the men could be imprisoned, family livestock and land title could be confiscated, or family members could be evicted.[126] From 1890s through 1920s, new taxes were imposed on Black men; the General Rate or poll tax and stock rate were good examples.[127] From 1897 onward, Quitrent was introduced. According to Redding, being registered as taxpayers qualified men as landholders and social adults—an experience that Black women never had.[128] As noted above, taxation policy was not only designed to keep Black women perpetually in minor status, but it was also designed to deny women all basic human rights.

Under the White minority government, Black women did not own land. In 1913, the White minority government enacted the Natives Land Act, which restricted Blacks to 13 percent of South African land.[129] Notably, the land reserved for Blacks under the above law was not only small, it was arid and lacked fertility.[130] On one level, the Natives Land Act played a major part in keeping Whites and non-White South Africans segregated. On another level, it was designed to prevent Africans from living off their land or reserves; thus, they were forced to supply cheap labor to the European industries, mines, and households in order to earn a living. Specifically, Black women, who typically farmed the land to provide food for their families, were forced to seek demeaning employment in White households as maids or domestic servants. Not only were they forced to receive meager pay, but working as domestic servants for White households underscored

---

126 Ibid., 61.
127 Ibid., 50.
128 Ibid., 49.
129 Jashodhara Tripathy, "Plight of Black Women in South Africa: Feminism Reinforced Sans Humanism" *Africa Quarterly*, v. 24, n. 3–4, 53.
130 Ibid., 53.

their triple subordination as being poor Black females living under a racist and sexist system.[131]

Significantly, Black women were voiceless primarily because the discrimination they suffered under White minority rule came from multiple sources. Tripathy notes that

> since they are women, many of their disabilities are not specific to black women but can be applied to women in general. Since they are Africans, many of their problems are not confined to women but are part of the overall discrimination to which all Blacks are subjected. Thus, as far as sufferings under the apartheid system are concerned, black women constitute a separate class.[132]

Phyllis Ntantala, a South African journalist, writes eloquently on behalf of these women as she describes their plight in the following words:

> It is the tragic story of thousands of young women who are widowed long before they reach the age of thirty; young married women who have never been mothers; young women whose life has been one long song of sorrow - burying one baby after another and lastly burying the husband. To them - both men and women - adulthood means the end of life; it means loneliness, sorrow, tears and death; it means a life without a future because there is no present.[133]

There was an underlying logic behind the series of draconian laws enacted by the White minority regime: each legal restriction imposed

---

131 Ibid., 52; Robert July, *A History of African People*, 445, 448; Helene Perold, *Working Women: A Portrait of South Africa's Black Women Workers* (Johannesburg: Ravan Press Ltd., 1985), 15.
132 Triparthy, "Plight of Black Women in South Africa," 52–53.
133 Ibid., 56.

on Black South Africans by this predatory system tore off an additional layer of their humanity. With the creation of the Native Affairs Act in 1920 and the Native Affairs Department in 1921, the government established an institutional mechanism for dealing with Blacks as a marginal entity.[134] Essentially, this arrangement was modeled after the British colonial administrative system of indirect rule, whereby local traditional political authorities handled routine administrative concerns on behalf of the colonial state at the local level. In the case of South Africa, the Native Affairs Department was the institutional channel through which the Pretoria regime exercised oversight over the affairs of the indigenous population.

Since many Blacks still resided in the urban centers, it became necessary to devise a way to confine them in the reserves in order to make this arrangement work. The opportunity to achieve that objective came with the worldwide influenza of the immediate post-World War I years, which was particularly severe in Black residential quarters (their living conditions were particularly poor due to lack of government interest in the health care of Africans), thus providing a much-needed pretext to promote segregation laws to the maximum. In 1921, the government set up the Native Affairs Commission.[135] Along with the Transvaal Local Government (the Stallard Commission) set up in 1922, the Native Affairs Commission was given the mandate to study the problems related to urban African settlement and accommodation.[136] Following a report submitted by the two committees, the government established the Natives (Urban Areas) Act of 1923, "which laid down the principle of residential segregation in the urban areas and reinforced the doctrine that Africans had no permanent rights in the towns and no justification in being there unless needed by whites as units of labor."[137]

Ultimately, the 1923 Act was designed to restrict Africans physically to the reserves, and to reserve the urban areas as much as possible for

---

134 Omer-Cooper, *History of Southern Africa*, 180.
135 Ibid., 169.
136 Ibid., 169.
137 Tripathy, "Plight of Black Women in South Africa," 58–63.

Whites. Toward this end, the government imposed limits on the amount of housing available to Black families in the urban areas. According to David Welsh, "segregation was defended on the grounds that Africans were 'primitive' and 'barbarous.'"[138] However, the truth of the matter is that the Europeans wanted African labor but not their presence. Commenting on the Natives (Urban Areas) Act, Tripathy suggests that the government recognized the homemaking role of the women, and feared that their presence in the cities would lead to the establishment of a stable Black urban population. Thus, trapped in the reserves, Black women held most of the responsibilities of maintaining the subsistence economy of their community. Since they also had to work in the urban centers as transient laborers, their social status declined while their workload doubled.[139] Since they were forced to maintain permanent residence in the reserves, African women had to endure most of the hardships associated with the environment. In addition to their daily chores in their homes and workplaces, Black women endured the loneliness occasioned by the constant absence of husbands, male friends, and male relatives and the brutality of street criminals and state security agents.[140]

It is particularly noteworthy that the Natives (Urban Areas) Act resulted in the massive forced removal of Africans from one location to another against their will, with the attendant emotional and physical trauma for Black families. In *The Surplus People: Forced Removals in South Africa*, the authors argue that the Group Areas Act was used to destroy many African settlements and African freehold settlements in the urban areas.[141] In her book *Strikes Have Followed Me All My Life,* Emma Mashinini, a Black labor unionist, recounts her childhood

---

[138] David Welsh, "The Growth of Towns" in Wilson and Thompson, *The Oxford History of South Africa*, v. 2, 188.

[139] Tripathy, "Plight of Black Women in South Africa," 54; Omer-Cooper, *History of Southern Africa*, 169.

[140] Tripathy, "Plight of Black Women in South Africa," 54.

[141] Laurine Platzky and Cherryl Walker, *The Surplus People: Forced Removals in South Africa* (Johannesburg: Raven Press, 1985), 100; Omer-Cooper, *History of Southern Africa*, 216–217.

experience with forced removal in the following words, "I attended the City Deep Methodist school in Heidelberg Road, Johannesburg, until 1936, when we suffered our first forced removal to make way for a white suburb. I was too young to remember much of our time there, but I do recall our home. . . ."[142] For many African children like Emma, the horror of the forced removal of their families by the White government left an indelible imprint on their memory. This was in sharp contrast to their White counterparts, who were privileged to live in beautiful, stable homes and residential areas. Considering the structure of the Black family at the time, it should be stressed that for the most part, Black mothers bore the burden of the forced relocation policy since they were the ones who kept their homes most of the time while the men worked as migrant laborers or languished in faraway prisons. The Natives (Urban Areas) Act remained in effect through the era of apartheid.

In 1927, the Hertzog government passed the Native Administration Act, which was aimed at tightening control on Africans outside the Cape.[143] As a result of this law, Blacks became increasingly vulnerable to police brutality and all manner of harassment in the cities. David Welsh states that a 1937 Police Commission of Inquiry found "abundant evidence that the enforcement by the police of the present law is often marked by unnecessary harshness, lack of sympathy and even violence."[144] As usual, police brutality knew no gender boundary. Black women were constantly awakened in the middle of the night with loud and violent knocks on their doors and windows, arrested and jailed, beaten up, and interrogated without any justification.[145] In some cases, the police coerced family members to reveal the whereabouts of their

---

142 Emma Mashinini, *Strikes Have Followed Me All My Life: A South African Autobiography* (New York: Routledge, 1991), 1.
143 Omer-Cooper, *History of Southern Africa*, 172.
144 Ibid., 200.
145 Winnie Mandela, *Part of My Soul Went With Him* (New York: W. W. Norton & Company, 1985), 23–24; Mashinini, *Strikes Have Followed Me All My Life*, 51.

relatives, thus subjecting them to the guilt of causing heavy pain to the latter.[146]

Commenting on the effects of the Native Administration Act, Welsh and Wilson state that

> nothing has done more to inflame African opinion than the pass laws. To Africans the pass is a symbol of servile status. If influx controls are to achieve their stated aims they must be strictly enforced. Strict enforcement, however, involves constant checks on Africans, carried out by "authorized officers," often taking the form of mass police raids on groups of Africans or townships. For example, between 1951 and 1962 an average of 339,255 Africans per year were convicted under various pass law offences.[147]

In 1927, the Hertzog government passed the Immorality Act to further its segregation agenda. This law "made sexual intercourse outside marriage between Whites and Africans a criminal offence."[148] The law was especially intended to protect the racial purity of the Afrikaner community.[149]

Black Women and Apartheid Laws

Following the electoral victory of the Nationalist Party in 1948, apartheid became the doctrinal capstone of the White minority government in South Africa. Apartheid, which means "separateness" in the Afrikaans language, came to be internationally used to designate South Africa's political doctrine, according to which different races

---

146 Makhoere, *No Child's Play*, 6.
147 Welsh, "The Growth of Towns" in Wilson and Thompson, *The Oxford History of South Africa*, v. 2, 200.
148 Omer-Cooper, *History of Southern Africa*, 172.
149 Ibid., 196.

must be kept apart from each other and allowed to develop along their cultural lines. Apartheid ideology was predicated on the claim "that every race has a unique destiny of its own and a unique contribution to make to the world."[150] This ideology was derived from an amalgam of South African practices, including the idea of racial superiority, Calvinist theology, and a certain amount of paternalistic philanthropy. Wheyl explains this when he states that "(the Boers) believed themselves to constitute a society of equals, consisting of people of the book — that is, the Old Testament — a spiritually elect element with a divine mission to accomplish on earth,"[151] and that "they considered themselves masters and in every respect the superiors of the non-white peoples among whom they lived."[152] Although there was no consensus within South Africa's religious community on apartheid, the system enjoyed considerable religious rationalization. For instance, in response to an interview conducted by June Goodwin, Mrs. Malan, the wife of National Party leader Dr. D. F. Malan, expressed the belief that the division of people into "groups" is God's way of averting human conflict, and argued that "the Bible says 'nations and the languages.'"[153] In light of such Afrikaner attitudes, it is not surprising that Thenjie Mtintso, a Soweto resident and friend of late Black nationalist Steve Biko, says that "on the whole, I'm fed up with Christianity. In South Africa, it's used to perpetuate slavery with such biblical injunctions as 'obey them that rule over you and submit yourself.'"[154]

Apartheid required that each racial group should have part of South Africa as a homeland. Significantly, the areas contemplated as homelands for the great majority of the total population of South Africa (the Blacks) or simply the native reserves, as stipulated by the Land

---

150 Susan P. Ogden, *Africa, South of Sahara* (Europa Publications, Ltd. London, 1986), 856.
151 Nathaniel Wheyl, *Traitor's End: The Rise and Fall of the Communist Movement in Southern Africa* (New York: Allington House, 1970), 27.
152 Ibid., 27.
153 June Goodman, "Christianity and Conflict in South Africa," *Christianity and Crisis* v. 44, n. 9 (May 28, 1984): 200.
154 Ibid., 202.

Acts, represented approximately 13 percent of South Africa's land mass, an area that was without significant industrial centers, major mineral deposits, or a major port.[155] Apartheid South Africa comprised four major racial groups that could actually be subdivided into smaller units. The national population of 28.7 million as of 1980 was distributed according to the following table.[156]

---

155 Ogden, *Africa*, 856.
156 Thompson, *A History of South Africa*, 278; Gary E. McCuen, *The Apartheid Reader: Ideas in Conflict Series* (Hudson, Wisconsin: Gary McCuem Publications Inc.,1986), 10.

TABLE 1

RACIAL COMPOSITION OF SOUTH
AFRICA'S POPULATION IN 1980

Group	Percentage	Population
Africans	72%	20.8m
Europeans	16%	4.5m
Colored	9%	2.6m
Asians	3%	0.8m
Total	100%	28.7m

A series of discriminatory laws was established in an effort to further entrench the structure of oppression in apartheid South Africa. In 1949, the nationalist government passed the Prohibition of Mixed Marriages Act, which outlawed interracial marriage. By preventing the possibility of further miscegenation among South Africa's multiracial groups, this law intended to further a fundamental Afrikaner agenda of preserving White racial purity.[157] Toward this end, the racist regime expanded the law to include marriages between Whites and Coloreds in 1950.[158] Also, in 1949, the government passed the Population Registration Act, which required that each South African be registered according to his or her racial category as determined by the apartheid government.[159] A major implication of this law for the Black community was its divisiveness. Generally this race-based system of classification was meant to reinforce the fundamental principle of differential treatment of different individuals and groups under apartheid rule. More to the point, the law had a negative impact on Black women, who were generally in charge of their families. Sometimes they were the direct victims of the government's arbitrary classification system. In *Cry Amandla*, June Goodwin describes how Thenjiwe Mtintso, a young female political activist, was forcefully separated from her family. Like her mother,

---

157 Omer-Cooper, *History of Southern Africa*, 196.
158 Ibid., 196.
159 Ibid., 196; Thompson, *A History of South Africa*, 190.

Thenjie was Xhosa in Soweto but was classified as a citizen of Transkei, the first tribal homeland to be declared an independent country by the apartheid regime.[160] Obviously, the ulterior motive behind the government's action was to neutralize this female activist by making it illegal for her to stay outside Transkei, the only area where there was less resistance to White minority rule at the time. Furthermore, Thenjie's case was intended to serve as a deterrence to other young women who were active in the anti-apartheid struggle.

In 1950, the government passed the Suppression of Communism Act and the Internal Security Act.[161] Under the Suppression of Communism Act, opponents of apartheid were automatically branded Communists and therefore enemies of the South African state. Further, the law was aimed at courting the United States and its European allies, who were involved in the Cold War with the former Soviet Union/Eastern Bloc. By presenting itself as a bulwark against communism in Southern Africa, the apartheid regime was able to deflect international pressure so that it could devote its energies to suppressing internal opposition. Like the men, Black female activists were indiscriminately arrested, detained, convicted, imprisoned, banished, and subjected to physical and verbal abuse once charged under one or a combination of the above laws. Winnie Mandela, the most arrested, detained, and banished Black woman in apartheid South Africa, discusses her ordeals in the hands of security agents. Between 1958 and 1985, she received several banning orders such as the one of 1962 described here:

> Under section 10(1)(a) of the Suppression of Communism Act, No. 44 of 1950, Winnie Mandela was required to abstain from any activity which might spread or promote any of the objects of "communism" in South Africa. "Receiving visitors" and having "social intercourse," for instance, are part of the long list of

---

160 Goodman, *Cry Amandla*, 17.
161 Winnie Mandela, *Part of My Soul*, 108–111; Thompson, *A History of South Africa*, 98–199; Omer-Cooper, *History of Southern Africa*, 202, 206.

prohibitions contained in the documents, in order to prevent the creation of an opportunity to "clandestinely conspire to engage in communist activities." In South Africa it is illegal to quote a banned person."[162]

Commenting on another situation when she was detained by security agents, Winnie Mandela said,

> I picked up that case. And then they said, "you are under arrest." There was the usual angry exchange. My daughter Zindzi was with me, and I wasn't prepared to leave her without exactly knowing how long I would be away. I never even had time to finish—I was whisked away, then I was taken to Protea police station. There they tried to interrogate me, but if you have been inside as long as I have, you cannot go through that worthless exercise again. No policeman can come to me today in my age and think that he can still interrogate me. In my younger days it was different, but any squeak of a little policeman who came to question me today would be wasting his time. We would just end up insulting each other, that's all. This went on for the rest of the morning till about ten o'clock.[163]

Winnie, a member of the ANC and the Federation of South African Women, was arrested, detained, imprisoned, banished, and banned about twenty-six times between 1958 and 1985. For example, in 1958, she was arrested for participating in the women's demonstration in Johannesburg against the issuing of passes to African women. She was imprisoned for two weeks. Winnie might have lost her first pregnancy in prison if other women who were imprisoned along with her had not intervened. Prominent among these women arrested and imprisoned

---

162 Winnie Mandela, *Part of My Soul*, 108.
163 Ibid., 24.

along with Winnie was Albertina Sisulu. In 1962, Winnie was accused of being a Communist and was banned for two years. She was restricted to Johannesburg. The following year, she was arrested for attending a gathering, but upon being found not guilty, the case was closed. In 1965, she was banned for five years. This caused her, her job with the Child Welfare Society. This became the pattern of her life and the lives of other women like her during the apartheid years.[164] One of the most common things that the anti-apartheid activists were accused of was being Communists. As mentioned earlier, the apartheid government took advantage of the Cold War conflict, posing as a strong ally of the West.[165]

One of the most far-reaching segregation measures taken by the apartheid regime, the Group Areas Act of 1950, empowered the authorities to evict Black, Colored, and Indian businesses from the Cape in favor of White businesses, using the zoning clause. As demonstrated by the passage below, the White minority regime seemed to have no qualms about carrying out its policy of segregation and racial purity in residential areas, business areas, religious gatherings, and schools.

> We make no apologies for the Group Areas Act, and for its application.
>
> . . . I think the world must simply accept it. The Nationalist Party came to power in 1948 and it said that it would implement residential segregation in South Africa
>
> . . . we put that Act on the Statute Book and as a result we have in South Africa, out of the chaos which prevailed when we came to power, created order and

---

164 Ibid., 106–108.
165 Thompson, *A History of South Africa*, 215.

established decent, separate residential areas for our people.¹⁶⁶

To strengthen the Native Land Act and Native (Group Areas) Act discussed earlier, the apartheid government passed the Prevention of Illegal Squatting Act in 1951. The latter law gave the Minister of Native Affairs power to relocate any African who was squatting or living on rural lands allocated to White farmers.¹⁶⁷ Under the above law, displaced Black tenants were to be resettled in camps built by local officials on the reserves. We have already mentioned the unique implications of lack of land relative to the social and economic well-being of Black women and their families. It is pertinent to add that the Prevention of Illegal Squatting Act was designed with an obvious intent to exacerbate their misery. In sharp contrast to the stable families, good residential quarters, jobs, and other rights and privileges enjoyed by their European counterparts in South Africa, these women and their families were being systematically reduced to illegal aliens in the only place they could call their homeland.

In 1953, three laws that would have a devastating impact on Black women and their families were passed by the apartheid regime: the Bantu Authorities Act, the Reservation of Separate Amenities Act, and the Bantu Education Act. According to Omer-Cooper, the Bantu Authorities Act "made provision for the establishment of local authorities in the reserves. These would be dominated by chiefs, whose powers were thus considerably increased. As chiefs were appointed by the government the increase in their powers was widely resented and the implementation of the legislation led to serious rural resistance."¹⁶⁸ Notably, the appointment of chiefs by the central government was intended to strengthen an earlier politico-administrative system of an indirect rule designed to advance the overarching agenda of racial

---

166 Senator P. Z. van Vuuren in Laurine Platzky and Cherryl Walker, *The Surplus People*, 100.
167 Omer-Cooper, *History of Southern Africa*, 199.
168 Ibid., 200.

separation and to tighten control on Blacks within the framework of local or homeland governments.

It is also noteworthy that under this arrangement "good" chiefs were expected to be responsive to the central government as opposed to the people. Not surprisingly, in sharp contrast with the precolonial era when traditional political leaders were elected from the royal families and were expected to rule with the aid of counselors who represented popular constituencies, these chiefs ruled with an iron hand like their "employers," and the result was local resistance. Monica Wilson states that by 1966 there were six territorial or district authorities: "Tswana, Lebowa (north Sotho), Matshangana (Tsonga), Thoho Ya Ndou (Venda), Transkei, and Ciskei."[169] Interestingly, these chiefs were all men. Thus, the Bantu Authorities Act reflected the patriarchal character of the apartheid system; African women were not recognized as leaders, hence only the men were appointed. Furthermore, because these chiefs had enormous political power, Black women continued to be marginalized politically even within the context of the territorial administrations. Third, this arrangement helped maintain Black women in underclass status since the majority of the women could not be appointed to salaried jobs, but could only serve the White families as domestic servants, nannies, and farm laborers. Ultimately, this legislation only confirmed the traditional thinking that "women should not be heard but should take orders from men."[170]

The Reservation of Separate Amenities Act and the Bantu Education Act strongly reinforced the bedrock of apartheid ideology, according to which racial groups were inherently unequal.[171] These laws offered a much-needed facade for the government's policy of providing unequal amenities to South Africa's diverse racial groups. For example, resources supplied to Black and White schools were provided qualitatively and

---

169 Wilson, "The Growth of Peasant Communities" in Wilson and Thompson, *The Oxford History of South Africa*, v. 2, 89.
170 Cherryl Walker, *Women and Resistance in South Africa* (London: Onyx Press Ltd, 1982), 125, 165, 205; Omer-Cooper, *History of Southern Africa*, 200, 208.
171 Omer-Cooper, *A History of Southern Africa*, 199.

quantitatively. While the government was spending a lot of money on White schoolchildren and making education compulsory for them, it did not make education compulsory for Black children, and it spent very little on Black schoolchildren.[172] To add salt to injury, the passage of the State Aided Institutions Act in 1957 legalized segregation in libraries, church services, theaters or entertainment centers, and sports, especially those sports where Black athletes generally performed better than their White counterparts.[173] For Black parents in general and Black mothers in particular, the government's actions suggested that regardless of their efforts and talents, Black children could never have the opportunity and resources to realize their potential in terms of athletic and educational pursuits. The White minority government was bent on exploiting their labor in a country that was generously endowed with human and natural resources. It is not surprising that prominent young Black activists like Thenjiwe Mtintso and the late Steve Biko were forced to drop out of medical school because their families were too poor to provide for their education.[174]

Perhaps the law that dealt the most deadly blow to the welfare of Black children was the Bantu Education Act of 1953, authored by the Minister of Native Affairs Dr. Verwoerd. To the great chagrin of Black parents in general and Black mothers in particular, this legislation denied Black children a quality educational system and opportunities in order to deny them quality employment opportunities in a White society.[175] Education policy under the apartheid system was based on the implicit assumption that Blacks needed just enough education to qualify them for unskilled and semi-skilled jobs. Thus, African education

---

172 Nelson Mandela, *Long Walk to Freedom: The Autobiography of Nelson Mandela* (Boston: Little, Brown and Company, 1994), 166–170; Thompson, *A History of South Africa*, 195–197, 201, 264–265; Gary E. McCuen, *The Apartheid Reader: Ideas in Conflict Series*, 37–39.
173 Ibid., 200.
174 Goodman, *Cry Amandla*, 13, 17–18.
175 Omer-Cooper, *History of Southern Africa*, 201; Wilson, "The Growth of Peasant Communities" in Wilson and Thompson, *The Oxford History of South Africa*, v. 2, 74–81.

ought to be calibrated to meet this objective.[176] Significantly, the Bantu education law required the Afrikaans language as the official language to be taught in Black schools. Black teachers, who were already poorly trained and poorly paid, were to work double shifts. Churches were required to adopt the new education policy in return for government subsidies or turn them over to the government, and they were divided over the policy: "With the exception of the Dutch Reformed Church, which supported apartheid, and the Lutheran mission, all Christian churches opposed the new measure."[177] While the Anglicans handed over their schools to the government, the Catholics kept theirs and sacrificed government subsidies.[178]

Nelson Mandela concurred with opponents of the Bantu Education Act when he argued that before 1948 the government was spending more money on White children's education but the syllabus was fairly the same. However, when Dr. Hendrick Verwoerd became the minister of Bantu education, racist education became stronger.[179] Arguing in defense of the government's policy, Dr. Verwoerd claimed that "education must train and teach people in accordance with their opportunities in life."[180] For many Black educators like Prof. Z. K. Matthews, "Education for ignorance and for inferiority in Verwoerd's schools is worse than no education at all."[181] The ANC responded by boycotting government-subsidized schools and providing alternative schools from April 1, 1955, the day the act would become effective. Unfortunately, ANC schools were not efficient, and the government continued to harass and sabotage its efforts. The alternative education project collapsed, and Black children were forced to return to apartheid

---

176 Omer-Cooper, *History of Southern Africa*, 201; Gary E. McCuen, *The Apartheid Reader: Ideas in Conflict Series*. (Gary E. McCuen Publications Inc., Hudson, Wisconsin, 1986), 12.
177 Omer-Cooper, *History of Southern Africa*, 167.
178 Ibid., 167.
179 Nelson Mandela, *Long Walk To Freedom*, 166.
180 Ibid. p. 167; David Mermelstein, *The Anti-Apartheid Reader: the Struggle Against White Racist Rule in South Africa* (New York: Grove Press, 1987), 180.
181 Nelson Mandela, *Long Walk to Freedom*, 167.

education. Eventually, the government's Bantu education policy led to school riots and the indiscriminate killing of Black schoolchildren by apartheid police, such as the Soweto Massacre in June 1976.[182]

The implications of the Bantu Education Act for Black women were numerous. In the first place, Black children were denied the educational opportunities of White kids. As Nelson Mandela rightfully puts it, "It is through education that the daughter of a peasant can become a doctor . . ."[183] Apartheid did not want Black children to receive a quality education that could enable them to graduate from perpetual poverty. For the millions of African children who grew up during apartheid, this was a dream that never came through: the dream to become whatever they wished to become. Second, Black women saw that their children were being miseducated but could not do anything about it. Inferior education and the Afrikaans language were being forced down their children's throats, but they had little or no power to immediately redeem the situation. Third, Black women had to deal with the fact that because their children had poorly trained and paid teachers, they were receiving inferior education, and authorities did not seem to care about what Black parents thought about the quality of education available to their children. Their children were being constantly harassed, arrested, tortured, or even killed by apartheid agents. Their children did not know the meaning of childhood but knew and experienced violence on a daily basis. Lastly, Black women had to fight apartheid along with their children to dismantle apartheid laws such as the Bantu Education Act. (This will be discussed in detail in chapter 4.)

Discrimination against Black women under the apartheid system took on a more specific and direct nature. As Tripathy points out, in terms of employment opportunities, Black women were the most disadvantaged group. Good jobs were usually reserved for men, either out of custom or on the basis of their presumed superior physical capabilities. Consequently, Black women were frequently hired as

---

182 Mermelstein, *The Anti-Apartheid Reader*, 183; *Women of South Africa: Their Fight for Freedom* (Boston: Little, Brown and Company, A Bulfinch Press Book, 1993), 132.
183 Nelson Mandela, *Long Walk to Freedom*, 166.

seasonal workers by White farmers, who often preferred to pay them in kind. In addition, by its very nature, seasonal work was not available on a regular basis.[184] Commenting on the fate of these women, Redding states that "simultaneously, they were to remain African or 'native' women who would not aspire to the same high social station as that held by White women."[185]

The labor tenancy system presented an enormous opportunity for white farmers to exploit Black laborers. Black families lived on White farms as renters, sharecroppers, or tenants and wage laborers. Like Africans under European rule, they were forced to accept very poor working conditions in order to earn money to pay taxes imposed on them by the White minority government. Chris Bauling, a White farmer, reportedly said the following to researcher Edith Jones about his relationship with his African laborers: "a few years ago my tenants came to me and said that they heard workers in Johannesburg got 2/6 a day. I said: 'You can have two and six a day if you work all the year round, 6 days a week, the full day. I will even give you your house plot, and I will feed you two meals on the working days, but you cannot have any land to plough, or stock.'"[186] The tenants involved in the above exchange refused the offer from a White farmer for the obvious reason that they did not want to give in to more economic exploitation. Yet, without land to cultivate, their case underscores the miserable condition in which most Black families lived during apartheid. Black laborers lived and worked in quasi-slavery conditions. In the words of Linda Waldman, "the labour conditions on the farms (the spider-webs) and the control exercised by farmers (the spiders) are discussed at some length in the literature . . . Farmers' actions and their relationship to farm workers have been characterised by the term 'paternalism.'"[187] Paternalism in the context of the relationship between the Afrikaner farmers and Africans

---

184 Tripathy, "Plight of Black Women in South Africa," 55.
185 Ibid., 58.
186 Stefan Schirmer, "What would we be without our Land and Cattle?": Migrations, Land, Labour Tenants in Mpumalanga, 1940–1950," *African Studies*, v. 55, n. 1 (1996): 113.
187 Waldman, "Monkey in a Spiderweb," *African Studies*, v. 55, n. 1, (1996): 64.

has been described as a quasi-kinship relationship between the two groups; the male head of the household (the Afrikaner farmer) exercised total control over the Black families employed on his farm. Under this arrangement, Black parents were more or less placed on the same level as their own children since the White landlord, or the patriarch, enjoyed the privilege of a man of legal standing, old enough to control the lives of his immediate family and his laborers.[188]

Black women who lived under these circumstances were usually subjected to physical and emotional abuses by White landlords, who enjoyed the full protection of the government and the apartheid system of justice. They were deprived of the joys of motherhood or the maternal authority that is taken for granted by every woman—the freedom to raise their children according to their cultural values. Notably, while White landlords had strict codes of conduct for adolescent Black girls, "both the farmer and residents believed that 'boys will be boys' and this sanctioned misbehavior and wildness in male youths."[189] This way, the system instilled antisocial behavior in Black male children, which often included tolerance of sexist conduct on their part. But also the racist system, in order to undermine the Black families and communities, did not want many responsible Black boys who would grow into responsible Black men; hence, many Black men grew up as alcohol addicts, wife and children abusers, lacking some basic responsibilities of fatherhood and basic respect for women.[190] Thus, apartheid therefore reinforced sexism in Black families. For example, some Black men wanted to control and dominate their families even when they were away from home on migrant labor contracts.

A major problem alluded to earlier is related to the precarious situation in which Black women found themselves and their families as a result of their husbands' long absences from home. By culture, South African Blacks attached a lot of value to land and cattle. Without their

---

188 Ibid., 65–66.
189 Ibid., 76.
190 Ibid.; Shahieda Issel, "Balancing Motherhood and Politics" in Diana E. H. Russell, *Lives of Courage: Women for a New South Africa* (New York: Basic Books, Inc., 1989), 68.

own land or livestock, many of the men could not face the humiliation of working on White farms or the poverty and malnutrition on the reserves. Their only hope for survival was to leave their families behind and migrate to the cities where they could get jobs as migrant laborers, with all the concomitant troubles. Typically, these men stayed away from home for long periods of time, and the women were left with the onerous burden of raising their children under very challenging conditions. As Elizabeth Gordon states, "the conditions are determined by South African law . . . the men leave their families behind in the villages and towns . . . as women and children are prohibited from living with a migrant worker . . ."[191] David Welsh adds that "a contract labourer cannot send for his family to join him in the town and he can never qualify under the law to do so."[192] Interestingly, not only did Black women have to contend with the patriarchal tendencies of the apartheid system, but also those of Black men who insisted on treating their spouses and fiancées as underlings. Despite the fact that the women shouldered the daily responsibilities of keeping their families together, Black men generally wanted to remain in control by making important decisions that the women were expected to implement.[193]

Under such circumstances, the conflict between Black women and men was inevitable, and the consequences for the Black family were often very dismal. Commenting on the social problems brought onto the Black community as a result of apartheid, Tripathy states that "the migrant labour system generates social chaos in the life of the African population, destroys families, leaves children without fathers, encourages alcoholism, prostitution and crime."[194] For example, some of the common problems associated with Black children included teenage pregnancies due to lack of parental supervision, such as in the case of Caeserina Makhoere, who became a parent and dropped out of

---

191 Elizabeth Gordon, "An Analysis of the Impact of Labour Migration on the Lives of Women in Lesotho," *Journal of Development Studies* (October 1980–July 1981), v. 17, 59.
192 David Welsh, "The Growth of Towns" in Wilson and Thompson, *The Oxford History of South Africa*, v. 2, 200.
193 Gordon, "An Analysis of the Impact of Labour Migration," 61.
194 Tripathy, "Plight of Black Women in South Africa," 56.

school at sixteen.[195] Some Black children became alcoholics, prostitutes, and got into all kinds of criminal activities. At the same time, since Black women had problems securing jobs, they turned to domestic service, which involved taking care of White households. Domestic service forced Black women to abandon their own children. While having domestic servants enabled Whites to devote "more time to their children's intellectual and emotional development,"[196] it meant that Black children were practically abandoned, both by their parents and the whole society.[197] White children were watched by Black nannies all the time. They had far greater chances of growing up in a stable and secure environment.[198] Some foreigners who visited South Africa during the apartheid years observed that Black women had no time to take good care of their families because of their domestic service to White families. For instance, June Goodman states that during one of her visits to South Africa, "I watched the last of the day-shift maids and cleaning women drift toward the bus and train stations for their journeys back to Soweto."[199] Jacklyn Cock describes the condition of service for these Black women as follows.

> Domestic workers are not protected by legislation stipulating the minimum wage, hours of work, or other conditions of service. Add to this legal vacuum the lack of disability and unemployment insurance, pensions and paid sick leave, and domestic workers are clearly an extremely insecure group of workers, open to exploitation by their employers. Such exploitation is evident, not only in their low wages, but also in the long hours they work.[200]

---

195 Makhoere, *No Child's Play*, 2.
196 Jacklyn Cock, *Maids and Madams: A Study in the Politics of Exploitation* (Johannesburg: Raven Press, 1980), 53.
197 Tripathy, "Plight of Black Women in South Africa," 60, 63.
198 Cock, *Maids and Madams*, 53.
199 Goodman, *Cry Amandla*, 14.
200 Cock, *Maids and Madams,* 41; Perold*, Working Women*, 30–40.

In *No Child's Play: In Prison Under Apartheid*, Caeserina Makhoere describes what it was like growing up under the apartheid system:

> My mother worked for a white family as a domestic and spent most of her time slaving for them. She was allowed only one day off every second Sunday. Every day she left home before sunrise and came back tired at sunset when it became dark; she was in no position to look after us. She was in no position to know what we were doing during the day. We had to look after ourselves and that created problems for us children. With no proper guidance we did whatever we liked; thus at 16 I became a mother.[201]

Yes, Black women took care of White children at the expense of their own children. In many cases such as the above, the consequence was teen pregnancy, and the girls involved were forced to drop out of school. Like their mothers, their employment opportunities were often limited to domestic service, which they had to accept in order to support their babies.[202] In fact, the more unfortunate Black dropout children like Caesarina often ended up in prison if they tried to challenge the system that was unfair to them.[203]

Another kind of job available to Black women was factory work. The women worked mainly in the clothing and food industries because "society defines this work as women's work." Making clothes and food seems like the work that women do at home.[204] Overall, about 4 percent of Black women were industrial workers, though it was not until the 1960s that factory jobs became available to Black women as a result of the economic boom that led to the construction of more factories.[205] As semi-skilled or unskilled workers, these women enjoyed some protection

---

201 Makhoere, *No Child's Play*, 2.
202 Cock, *Maids and Madams*, 54.
203 Makhoere, *No Child's Play*, 6–12.
204 Ibid., 56.
205 Perold, *Working Women*, 16.

that was not available to domestic servants. However, they were usually underpaid in comparison to men or other women (Indian, Colored, and White) performing similar tasks.[206] For example, in the Transvaal area, a male sewing machinist made ZAR 27.50, while a Black female made ZAR 22.00 for the same job.[207] A 1964 survey revealed that the average monthly pay for Black female factory workers was ZAR 35.68, while that of their male counterparts was ZAR 65.54.[208]

About 3 percent of Black women did professional work, mainly as teachers, nurses, social workers, and rarely as lawyers and medical doctors.[209] The women were recruited to teach in the African schools because Dr. Verwoerd believed they were better at handling children, and their salaries would save the government some money.[210] The salary paid to a Black teacher was 67 percent of the salary paid to a White counterpart. In 1954, Dr. Verwoerd tried to explain this inequity by saying that

> the salaries which European teachers enjoy are in no way a fit or permissible criterion for the salaries of Bantu teachers. The European teacher is in service of the European community and his salary is determined in comparison with the income of the average parent whose children he teaches. . . . In precisely the same way the Bantu teacher serves the Bantu community and his salary must be fixed accordingly.[211]

Another observer states that "the teachers teaching in schools for African students are ill-trained. Of the 70,195 African women teachers in 1978, only 21 percent had teaching qualifications as well as a degree, less than 15 percent of them had completed high school, although most

---

206 Ibid., 16; Tripathy, "Plight of Black Women in South Africa," 61.
207 Tripathy, "Plight of Black Women in South Africa," 62.
208 Perold, *Working Women*, 54.
209 Ibid., 19, 23, 46.
210 Tripathy, "Plight of Black Women in South Africa," 64.
211 Ibid., 65.

of them had not undergone teacher training courses. The vast majority of them had no formal education beyond standard VIII."[212] Not only were Black teachers poorly prepared for their job, they were overworked and underpaid. Catherine, a female schoolteacher, states that "I started being a teacher in 1980. Since I started, I've taught all subjects. Even now. Really, the problem I meet is a matter of the subjects which were difficult for me at school."[213]

Black nurses had their own share of discrimination in apartheid South Africa. To begin with, as nurses, Black women were not allowed to become married, and they immediately lost their jobs if they went against this rule.[214] Second, the government protected White nurses by passing the so-called Nursing Act of 1957, which stipulated that "no non-white nurse may be elected to the Nursing Council as Nursing Association, but the membership and payment of contribution to the Association was compulsory for all."[215] Furthermore, because of segregation laws, the council provided separate training for White and non-White nurses. To make matters worse, apartheid made it a criminal offense for a non-White nurse to supervise a White nurse regardless of the individual's qualifications and experience. The punishment for this offense was a $400 fine.[216]

As a result of apartheid laws, the health-care delivery system in the reserves was grossly inadequate. As a result, Black women faced peculiar health problems; many suffered from prolonged health problems, including mental illness and hypertension.[217] Pregnant Black women and children suffered from malnutrition; moreover, Black women were frequently dismissed from their jobs if they became pregnant, and many were forced into dangerous abortion procedures to avoid losing their jobs. The government's solution was compulsory birth control, which was not

---

212 "Oppression of Black Women in Apartheid South Africa," *The Ethiopian Herald*, 30 September 1981.
213 Catherine's interview in 1984 in Perold, *Working Women*, 48.
214 Tripathy, "Plight of Black Women in South Africa," 65.
215 Ibid., 65.
216 Ibid., 65.
217 Ibid., 68.

applied to White women. The United States-manufactured birth control injection Depo-Provera was made available to Black women in South Africa even though it was generally believed in the western world that this medicine was causing cancer.[218] The implications of all of this were clear. First, the apartheid government did not care about high infant mortality rates in Black communities. For example, between 1956 and 1960 the infant mortality rate for Black people was 116 per 1,000 live births, but 30 per 1,000 live births for Whites.[219] The reason for the gap was the quality of medical facilities available for each group. Second, the apartheid government did not want high birth rates and population growth for Blacks because the majority Black population was a threat to the racist system. Third, they did not care about the high mortality rate or deadly illnesses among Black women because they had no interest in protecting the lives of Black people. Instead, the system aimed at destroying Black people and their communities. Finally, apartheid was a systematic racist system that also aimed at making South Africa a country for only Europeans.

Conclusion

Although apartheid was formally instituted in 1948, the racist system had been in place since 1652, the year the Dutch East India Company decided to establish a "service station" at the Cape. Apartheid had only gone through different phases, as discussed in this chapter. During the period 1910 through 1947, the White minority government consolidated its power through a series of constitutional and legislative actions that formed the immediate backdrop to apartheid; during the period 1948 through 1994, the term *apartheid* was adopted by Pretoria as a designation for one of the most racist systems of governance in modern times. As mentioned earlier, the Natives Land Act of 1913 restricted Africans, about 72 percent of the total population, to only

---

218 Ibid., 67.
219 Thompson, *A History of South Africa*, 279.

about 13 percent of the land. Africans could only live in this 13 percent of the land called *the reserves*. At the same time, the Europeans had a lot of land for expansion and development. Other building blocks to apartheid included the Native Affairs Act of 1920, the Native Affairs Commission of 1921, the Native Administration Act of 1927 and the Immorality Act also of 1927, Natives (Urban Areas) Act and the Natives (Urban Areas) Amendment Act of 1923 and 1930 respectively, the Natives Trust and Land Act of 1936, Native Representation Act of 1936, Native Laws Amendment Act of 1937, and so on.

Before and throughout the apartheid era, Black women were the victims of various forms of oppression in South Africa. Among other things, they were treated as legal minors. Consequently, they could not sue anyone, represent themselves or testify in courts of law. From a legal standpoint, Black women could not own homes or be recognized as adults and heads of their families. They were harassed, arrested, beaten, banned, imprisoned, relocated, raped, forced into exile, or even killed for protesting their conditions. Black women were not allowed to live in the urban areas except when they had to work for White families, who typically addressed them as "maids." These women endured the hardship of raising their children and looking after older members of their families alone because their husbands had been forced into exile, killed, or had to be away from their families as migrant laborers. Black women and their families did not have access to good housing, education, employment, and good health care. As a result, they lived in extreme poverty with the attendant problems of malnutrition, high mortality rate, civil rights abuse, illiteracy, and lack of skills, to mention but a few. As a result of their dismal experience with White minority rule, Black women could not be left out of the anti-apartheid struggle. They paid a heavy price individually and collectively for challenging apartheid. The next chapter focuses on their contributions to the long drawn-out effort to dismantle the racist system.

CHAPTER 4

Black Women's Response To Apartheid

Women also led the massive anti-pass campaigns that erupted across South Africa in the mid - '50s. A UN publication describes some of these courageous actions: "On 9 August 1956, in a protest organized by FSAW (Federation of South African Women), more than 20,000 women came to the Union Buildings in Pretoria to see the Prime Minister. When he refused to see them, they placed petitions with more than 100,000 signatures in his office. . . ."[220]

—Gary E. McCuen

Violence is not restricted to men — women are becoming increasingly more militant. However, Lloyd Vogelman, the director of the Witwatersrand's Research Project on Violence, believes women engaged in violence as a desperate last resort. "Women feel that unless they destroy the enemy, their lives and those of their family would be seriously jeopardized," he says. He points out that with traditional structure broken down, women find themselves in the unaccustomed role of head of

---

220 Gary E. McCuen, *The Apartheid Reader: Ideals in Conflict Series*, (Hudson, Wisconsin: Gary McCuen Publications Inc. 1986), 35.

the household, with the added duties of protecting and defending, not a normal role for black women.[221]

—Lioyd Vogelman

You who have no work, speak. You who have no homes, speak. You who have no schools, speak. You who have to run like chickens from the vulture, speak. Let us share our problems so that we solve them together. We must free ourselves. Men and women must share housework. Men and women must work together in the home and out in the world. There are no crèches and nursery schools for our children. There are no homes for the aged. There is no-one to care for the sick. Women must unite to fight for these rights. I opened the road for you. You must go forward.[222]

—Dora Tamana

Introduction

THIS CHAPTER IS organized into two principal parts. Part one discusses the history of some anti-apartheid organizations in which Black women were involved, with particular reference to specific incidents that led to the formation of each organization, and specific aspects of apartheid policies that were challenged by these organizations. Other issues examined in this part include the strategies employed by the female activists as well as the outcomes of their struggle.

---

221 Lloyd Vogelman in Carol Lazar, *A Single Photograph, a Thousand Words* (Boston: Little, Brown and Company Inc. A Bulfinch Press, 1993), 99–100.
222 Dora Tamana in *To Honor Women's Day: Profiles of Leading Women in the South African and Namibian Liberation Struggles* (Cambridge, MA: International Defence and Aid Fund for Southern Africa in Co-operation with United Nations Centre Against Apartheid, August 1981), 40.

Part two discusses the leadership roles of a selected number of Black women in the context of the anti-apartheid organization in which the women were involved.

To begin with, readers are reminded that although the apartheid regime played the color card as part of its divide-and-rule strategy, all the non-European women involved in anti-apartheid activities—the Africans, Asians, and Colored—collectively refer to themselves as "Black women."[223] Therefore, the use of the term in this chapter continues to reflect such inclusive identification. It is also important to remind readers that although this work focuses on Black women, many European-African women like Helen Joseph and members of the Black Sash fought apartheid and paid a high price for their anti-apartheid activities. Finally, it is necessary to point out that other groups such as South African students, churches, and workers made major contributions to the struggle to dismantle apartheid. In *A History of South Africa,* Leonard Thompson states that "Because most secular anti-apartheid leaders were in exile, in prison, or banned, the clergy were thrust into the fore of the struggle against apartheid. Especially prominent [was] Desmond Tutu . . ."[224] For example, during the 1988 elections, a group of clergy from the South African Council of Churches and sixteen other denominations led a massive boycott of the June 1988 elections, insisting that "By involving themselves in the elections, Christians would be participating in their oppression or the oppression of others."[225] Even Black schoolchildren took up arms against apartheid, whose draconian policies did not spare the most vulnerable members of society. In *A Single Photograph, A Thousand Words,* Carol Lazar shows a photograph taken by Peter Magubane of young schoolgirls "who changed the course of the history of South Africa when they rose in defiance of apartheid rule on June 16, 1976."[226] Thus, the contributions

---

223 Diane E. H. Russell, *Lives of Courage: Women in a New South Africa* (New York: Basic Books, Inc. Publishers, 1989), 6, 11.
224 Leonard Thompson, *A History of South Africa* (New Haven: Yale University Press, 1995), 239.
225 Ibid., 239.
226 Lazar, *A Single Photograph,* 101.

made by women in the struggle against apartheid must be seen in the context of a collaborative effort.

Margaret Mackay observed that "the South African people have waged a long determined struggle for liberation - and in that struggle, women have played a central role. The role of female activists in the struggle was also acknowledged by the predominantly male leadership of the struggle. For instance, in 1984 the African National Congress president, Oliver Tambo said that "In our beleaguered country, the women's place is in the battle front of struggle." Declaring that year the "Year of the Women," he added that "Perhaps the fact that Black women are the most heavily oppressed by the apartheid system—on the basis of their race, their class, and their sex—explains why they have opposed it with such courage and determination."[227]

Significantly, although Black women were often asked by their male counterparts to leave "politics" or "words" to the men in keeping with the local tradition (see chapter 2), they were invariably caught in the struggle. After all, as acknowledged by Oliver Tambo, they were the worst hit by the racist regime. As Mackay comments,

> This system scars the life of every Black South African - but women bear the brunt of it. Many South African women must struggle alone to support children and aged relatives on the barren reserves, apart from husbands and fathers who have sought work in the cities. Others driven by the need to earn a living must leave their children behind and move illegally to the urban areas in search of work. An intricate series of laws prevents them from settling in the cities. Most women are faced daily with the possibility of being "repatriated" to the area where they were born, or to a "homeland" they have never seen, or removed to resettlement camps.[228]

---

227 Margaret Mackay, quoted in McCuen, *The Apartheid Reader*, 32.
228 Ibid., 32.

In *Part of My Soul Went with Him,* Winnie Mandela recounts her experience with a series of forced relocations while her husband, Nelson, was in prison. Her experience shows how the relocation policy was used to neutralize strong female opponents of apartheid. Armed security men would usually knock on her door very early in the morning, arresting her on a trumped-up charge and forcing her to leave for an unknown destination. In one occasion, Winnie was removed from Orlando and banished to Bradfort. She describes her experience with the security agents as follows.

> We were taken into one of these army trucks. Our every possession was there: they had ripped off bedspreads and sheets from the bed, they took everything, emptied the wardrobes and cupboards into these sheets, my crockery was tied up with the blankets, three quarters of course was broken into pieces, Nelson's books were bundled into bedspreads. Of course half of the stuff got damaged.[229]

Commenting on the horror to which her sixteen-year-old daughter, Zindzi, was subjected in the course of this particular experience, Winnie further states that

> it was terrible. For Zindzi it was a traumatic experience. Any man could have been broken by that type of thing. It was calculated to do just that. Worse things have happened to people in the struggle, but for a sixteen-year-old girl it was very hard to take. It was the hardest thing for me to take as a mother, that your commitment affects those who are dear to you. That shattering

---

[229] Winnie Mandela, *Part of My Soul Went with Him* (New York: W. W. Norton & Company, 1965), 25.

experience inflicted a wound that will never heal. Of course I was bitter, more than I've ever been.[230]

The traumas imposed on the Mandela family were also imposed on many families through forced removals. In the case of Sophiatown, located close to Johannesburg, all African families were removed by force between 1955 and 1963 and the area given to Whites. The Natives Areas Act (one of the most potent instruments of White domination) not only empowered the government to relocate African families by force, but it allowed new White settlers to de-Africanize the identities of towns previously inhabited by Blacks. In this case, Sophiatown, which was founded by a distinguished Black doctor, Dr. Xuma, was renamed *Triomf,* an Afrikaner word for triumph.[231] Of course, Africans usually resisted the policy, but they could not match the brute force of an autocratic regime that had little respect for Blacks. For instance, the nonviolent protest staged by the Black community of Sophiatown was violently crushed by a 2,500 strong contingent of security agents deployed by the apartheid regime to enforce its will.[232] The town was promptly transferred to White families and the Africans were moved to Meadowlands, about fifteen to twenty miles farther away from Johannesburg. Don Mattera, a Black South African poet who used to be a resident of Sophiatown, summed up the determination of these Black families to survive:

> Memory is a weapon. I knew deep down inside of me, in that place where laws and guns cannot reach nor jackboots trample, that there had been no defeat. In another day, another time, we would emerge to reclaim

---

230 Ibid., 32.
231 Emma Mashinini, *Strikes Have Followed Me All My Life: A South African Autobiography* (New York: Routledge, 1991), 4.
232 Nelson Mandela, *Long Walk to Freedom, The Autobiography of Nelson Mandela* (Boston: Little, Brown and Company, 1994), 122,153–156, 164–166, 203.

our dignity and our land. It was only a matter of time and Sophiatown would be reborn.[233]

Nomazizi Sokudela, a member of the ANC Women's League, also observed that "Women were the most oppressed of the Black majority, and perhaps that explains why women have been in the forefront of the liberation struggle."[234] She made a connection between the struggle against apartheid and the struggle for gender equality at the national level. Women saw apartheid laws that made them perpetual minors as worth fighting against. They wanted to enter into contracts without help from men; they wanted to own or dispose of property; they wanted to serve as legal guardians for their children. Thus, as will be discussed in the next chapter, from the standpoint of the women, victory against apartheid must also be measured in terms of how power is shared between men and women in every aspect of life in post-apartheid South Africa.

The women formed anti-apartheid organizations through which they articulated issues and concerns that were of particular interest to them and their families. These include the African National Congress Women's League (ANCWL), the Federation of South African Women (FSAW), African Women's Association (AWA), the Black Sash, and the Domestic Workers Union, to mention but a few. Black women were also members of or worked closely with the following inclusive anti-apartheid organizations: the African National Congress (ANC); Azanian People's Organization (AZAPO); the Black Consciousness Movement; Congress of South African Trade Unions (COSATU); the Commercial, Catering and Allied Workers' Union of South Africa (CCAWUSA); United Democratic Front (UDF); the South African Indian Congress; the End Conscription Campaign (ECC); the South African Communist Party; and a host of others.

For the purpose of illustration, the following organizations are discussed in detail in the subsequent sections of this chapter: the

---

233 Don Mattera quoted in Mashinini, *Strikes Have Followed Me All My Life*, 4.
234 Nomazizi Sokudela quoted in McCuen, *The Apartheid Reader*, 34.

African National Congress (the ANC), Federation of South African Women (FSAW), the Commercial, Catering and Allied Workers' of South Africa (CCAWUSA), United Democratic Front (UDF), and the Black Consciousness Movement. With the exception of the Black Consciousness Movement, the rest of the above organizations were inclusive as membership was not confined to any particular race, gender, class, or age. Although an organization such as the ANC had restricted membership requirements at its formation in 1912, it worked closely with other anti-apartheid organizations like the South African Communist Party (SACP) and the South African Indian Congress (SAIC).[235] As a matter of fact, people could choose to be members of both the ANC and the SACP.[236] The Black Consciousness was mainly for young Black people while the ANC was a more diverse organization when it later on decided to give women and other non-Africans full membership in the organization. While the decision to look at the above organizations is aimed at highlighting the collective contributions of Black women toward the struggle against apartheid, the leadership of four prominent women—Winnie Mandela, Emma Mashinini, Nontsikelelo Albertina Sisulu, and Thenjiwe Mtintso—are given special attention.

Profiles

Winnie Mandela

Winnie Mandela is discussed in the context of her active roles in the African National Congress (the ANC), the African National Congress Women's League (ANCWL), and the Federation of South African Women (FSAW). As mentioned in chapter 2, the South African Native Congress was formed in 1912 in response to the formation of a

---

[235] Nelson Mandela, *Long Walk to Freedom*, 91, 115–116; Leo Kuper, *Passive Resistance in South Africa* (New Haven: Yale University Press, 1957), 13, 99; June Goodman, *Cry Amandla: South African Women and the Question of Power* (New York: Africana Publishing Company, 1984), 44.
[236] Goodman, *Cry Amandla*, 194.

segregated Union of South Africa two years earlier.[237] This organization was later renamed the African National Congress or the ANC.[238] Under the leadership of African men like Dr. Pixley Seme, Sol T. Plaatje, and others, the ANC "sought full African citizenship through the franchise and the end of restrictions on landholding and personal movement."[239] The ANC became the most popular organization in the struggle to dismantle apartheid during the second half of the century as it challenged every law or legislation designed to ensure White political and economic dominance under the apartheid system. Unfortunately, while the ANC was formed to fight for human rights in the Union of South Africa and later on in apartheid South Africa, it denied women full membership during its early years, and its discrimination against women resulted in the formation of the African National Congress Women's League (ANCWL) in 1943. Madie-Hall Xuma was its first president.[240] As mentioned in chapter 1, not only did Black women have to struggle against apartheid policies that were, at the same time, racist and sexist, they also struggled against gender-based discrimination within their own communities. With the formation of the ANC Women's League, "there was a new awareness at work — the awareness that the experience of women under apartheid demanded its own voice. Women emerged at the forefront as political leaders."[241]

Women activists operating within the framework of the ANCWL and FSAW engaged in protest activities like their male counterparts in the ANC. Winnie Mandela held important positions in both organizations. According to her own account, "I held the same positions in the Federation of South African Women as I had in the ANC Women's League: I was chairlady of our branch and I belonged to

---

237 Robert July, *A History of the African People* (Prospect Heights, Illinois: Waveland Press, Inc. 1998), 363; Thompson, *A History of South Africa*, 156.
238 July, *A History of the African People*, 363.
239 Ibid., 363, 454–455.
240 Lazar, *A Single Photograph*, 34.
241 Ibid.

the provincial executive and national executive."[242] As "a powerful personality and leader in her own right, with an extraordinarily strong and regal presence, Winnie acknowledged and respected many women like Lilian Ngoyi, Helen Joseph, Albertina Sisulu, Florence Matomela, Frances Baard, Kate Molale, and Ruth Mompati who had influenced her political life."[243] Through her acknowledgment of these women's contributions, she reinforces our appreciation for the collective nature of the women's effort to resist apartheid policies. For Winnie, during those long and difficult years, these women "were just a continuation of Nelson."[244]

Winnie helped organize some anti-pass demonstrations in 1958 and, like many Black women involved in this effort, she was pregnant with her first baby. She was among thousands of women arrested during the unrest. Her friend Albertina Sisulu, who was a nurse, "saved my first baby," when Albertina "went out of her way in prison to look after me."[245] In spite of all the restrictions apartheid imposed on Winnie and other Black female activists, they were involved in numerous less explicitly political causes and organizations such as Margaret Ballinger's home for blind and deaf children,[246] the Black Women's Federation, and the Black Parents' Association in Soweto.[247] These organizations helped to address specific concerns of Black women that derive from apartheid policies while fostering a spirit of oneness among them and their families. For example, during the May 1976 launching of the BPA, Winnie exhorted Black parents to support their schoolchildren in their protests against Bantu education and the shooting of unarmed schoolchildren by the apartheid security agents. Commenting on the Afrikaans issue, she stated that "we must not let the children fight their

---

[242] Winnie Mandela, *Part of My Soul*, 66; Winnie Mandela, "A Leader in Her Own Right" in Russell, *Lives of Courage*, 97.
[243] Russell, *Lives of Courage*, 95.
[244] Winnie Mandela, *Part of My Soul*, 66.
[245] Ibid., 67; Winnie Mandela, "A Leader in Her Own Right" in Russell, *Lives of Courage*, 105.
[246] Ibid., 67.
[247] Russell, *Lives of Courage*, 97.

battle for us, they must have our support . . . what the children learn in school is also our responsibility. If we let them down now, they will spit on our graves one day."[248] At this time, the Bantu education policy had provoked Black schoolchildren who did not want to be taught in Afrikaans. On June 16, 1976, the children's protest against their racist curriculum was met with state-sponsored violence that killed hundreds of protesters. The next day, June 17, the schoolchildren responded to the killings of their friends with riots in Soweto.[249]

To Winnie and many fellow Black mothers, this situation was obviously not acceptable and they could not be silenced. Although the June 16, 1976, protest was not spearheaded by specific individuals, the government took to its usual tactics of looking for scapegoats, and Winnie was a favorite target.[250] Her offense was that she helped to organize the Black Parents Association, which attracted people—including religious leaders, social workers, and parents, to mention a few—from all over the country to form a resource group for the victims of the Soweto shooting. A lot of needs were to be met, including procuring funds for the victims' families, arranging mass burials, preparing food, and caring for orphans. The government responded by confiscating the sum of ZAR 194,000 that was donated to the victims of its terrorist tactics.[251] Then, when Winnie and Bishop Buthelezi went to the Protea Police station to complain about the shootings at the demonstrators, Mayor Visser accused her of starting the riots and then coming to the authorities after the situation got out of control. Winnie responded by throwing things at him and shouting, "You bloody murderer, killer of our children, and you tell us we started the riots. You go and stop those bastards killing our children in the street!"[252] Winnie was arrested and imprisoned along with about a dozen women. To say the least, those women were subjected to physical and psychological

---

248 Winnie Mandela, *Part of My Soul*, 115.
249 Ibid., 114.
250 Ibid., 115.
251 Ibid.
252 Dr. Nthatho Motlana in Winnie Mandela, *Part of My Soul*, 115–116.

trauma by security agents. For example, they were not allowed to wear panties, stockings, and shoes. Because the authorities perceived her as the ringleader, Winnie was subsequently banished to Brandfort for nine years, an isolated, conservative, Afrikaner community so as to "contain her troubles."[253]

Some of the unique leadership qualities Winnie displayed are worth special mention. Although she was a prominent actor in the movement, her activities were generally confined to the grassroots level. As a result of her background as a social worker, she easily identified with ordinary people.[254] It is particularly noteworthy that instead of succumbing to its intimidation, the racist system turned her into a very strong woman who was willing to risk much of what was dear to her in order to realize the collective dreams of her dispossessed people.[255] Her family members and friends also received their own dose of brutalization at the hands of apartheid authorities on account of their relationship with her or their support for her and her family during the apartheid period. For example, her sister, who was very close to her, died in Botswana as an expatriate.[256] Despite her ever-present predicaments, Winnie refused to give up the struggle through to the end of apartheid.

Nontsikelelo Albertina Sisulu

Albertina Sisulu, or Mama Sisulu as she is fondly known, is the mother of seven children (five biological children and two adopted children) and the wife of Walter Sisulu, Nelson Mandela's close associate.[257] As the secretary general of ANC from 1949, her husband played a key role in the anti-apartheid struggle. Walter Sisulu was detained several

---

253 Sally Motlana in Winnie Mandela, *Part of My Soul*, 116; *To Honor Women's Day*, 14–16.
254 Russell, *Lives of Courage*, 97.
255 Winnie Mandela, "A Leader in Her Own Right" in Russell, *Lives of Courage*, 105; Winnie Mandela, *Part of My Soul*, 115–117.
256 Winnie Mandela, "A Leader in Her Own Right" in Russell, *Lives of Courage*, 105.
257 Nontsikelelo Albertina Sisulu, "Co-President of the United Democratic Front" in Russell, *Lives of Courage*, 147–151.

times before he was imprisoned for life with Nelson Mandela at Robin Island.[258] Like Winnie Mandela, Albertina was a staunch anti-apartheid activist who would not give up the struggle despite the government's effort to undercut her determination by literally destroying her marriage by depriving her family of the economic and emotional support of her husband and the father of her children.

Albertina joined the ANCWL shortly after she married Walter. For her, Black women were the hardest hit by apartheid and needed their own forum for discussing issues important to women, such as low salaries, passes for women, high cost of living, maternity leave, and children's education.[259] For example, she wanted to participate in the 1952 Defiance Campaign but had to stay home with their little children since Walter was participating. Since she was not directly participating in the campaign, she "helped feed the families of the people in jail."[260] This extraordinary woman believed that "women are the people who are going to relieve us from all this oppression and depression. The rent boycott that is happening in Soweto now is alive because of the women. It is the women who are on the street committees educating the people to stand up and protect each other."[261]

Like Winnie Mandela and many Black women in apartheid South Africa, Albertina was forced to raise her children alone since her husband was in and out of jail and eventually imprisoned for life. Therefore, she did not have a normal family life. A nurse and a midwife by profession, she also had very negative experiences with the apartheid system during her training in a non-European hospital (the Johannesburg hospital was only for Europeans). During her years as a practicing nurse, she made the telling discovery that regardless of her training and experience, a Black nurse under apartheid could not be entrusted with managerial responsibilities.[262]

---

258 Russell, *Lives of Courage*, 144; *To Honor Women's Day*, 38.
259 Sisulu in Russell, 147.
260 Ibid., 147–148.
261 Ibid., 143.
262 Ibid., 146, 148; *To Honor Women's Day*, 38.

In 1954, Albertina helped found the Federation of South African Women. She and her colleagues wanted an organization that would include women from diverse backgrounds—churchwomen, trade union women, women from different racial and ethnic groups, socioeconomic classes, or age categories. As cofounder and third president of the organization, she played a key role in the anti-apartheid movement, which included her efforts in helping organize the 1958 anti-pass demonstration by the FSAW. Specifically, she led the second batch of women to the pass office. Commenting on their activities during this historic occasion, she said that "we went to the pass office with duplicate passes, which we'd tear up; then we'd drive the women out of the pass office."[263] In keeping with the intimidation strategy of the apartheid regime, Albertina and many of her coprotesters were arrested and locked up in jail for three weeks. At the time, she was still breastfeeding a ten-month-old baby, who had to be taken care of by her mother-in-law. She became sick as a result of her forced separation from her baby.[264]

Although Albertina was sick in jail, she had time to reach out to other women who were also having some difficulties. As an experienced mother and nurse, she helped save Winnie's first baby by demanding that she be taken to the hospital. Albertina did more by protesting against the inhumane treatment given to nonpolitical prisoners. She and her friends became very angry when they saw the terrible conditions in jail, such as the indiscriminate whipping of the prisoners during their routine hard manual labor. At one time they argued with the prison authorities that "these people are punished enough. They shouldn't be assaulted as well."[265] Like many anti-apartheid activists, Albertina was accused of being a Communist, and in 1963 spent three months in jail under the Suppression of Communism Act. Like Winnie she was also banned from political activities and placed under house arrest for several years. In spite of the government's effort to silence her, Albertina routinely spoke at funeral ceremonies, and her public engagements

---

263 Ibid., 148.
264 Paula Hathorn, "The End Conscription Campaign" in Russell, *Lives of Courage*, 158.
265 Sisulu in Russell, *Lives of Courage*, 149.

invariably earned her several jail terms as the authorities accused her of using such occasions to promote the goals of an illegal organization, the ANC. For instance, in 1981 she was sentenced to a three-year jail term for violating state law when giving a eulogy in honor of coactivist Rose Mbele while the ANC's flag was flying.[266]

Ironically, although she was always in and out of jail, or perhaps because of that, she was highly respected by the people in the struggle. Thus, while still serving a jail sentence in 1983, she was elected president of the Transvaal branch of the United Democratic Front (UDF).[267] Notably, Albertina was involved in the effort to establish the UDF to fill the vacuum that resulted from the government's decision to ban ANC and other anti-apartheid organizations in the 1960s. Following the ban, there was a need to form another organization that would assume the role of educating the people on the issues relating to apartheid. According to Albertina, "Before UDF, everybody was standing on their own. It was formed to unite the people and give them a direction, and it worked wonderfully. Now when we have boycotts, we speak with one voice. Even more than unity, people needed to understand who the enemy is. For example, the government says the ANC is a terrorist organization. We explain to people that the real terrorist is the government."[268] Like other pioneers of the anti-apartheid movement, Albertina helped to educate the people on the nature of the apartheid system and why it should be dismantled. This kind of political education went a long way in keeping the names of ANC's imprisoned leaders like Nelson Mandela and Walter Sisulu in the minds of the people, and ultimately kept the spirit of the struggle alive.

Albertina also spoke against the brutalities and other crimes committed by apartheid security agents. For instance, she was very critical of the government's decision in 1985 to send soldiers into Black communities, a decision that resulted in the cold-blooded murder of innocent Black children. Recounting the above incident, she said that

---

266 Ibid., 150; *To Honor Women's Day*, 39.
267 Ibid., 151.
268 Ibid.

"children would be playing in the playgrounds, and the soldiers would tell them to disperse. When the children were running in all directions, they were shot in their backs like wild animals."[269] Concerned with the series of killings of Black children since the Soweto Uprisings in 1976, she took her protest to White suburban residents, especially White women whom she expected to be sympathetic as mothers. With characteristic bluntness, Albertina placed the responsibility for the killings at the door of her White sisters by saying, "our children are dying in the townships, killed by your children. You are mothers. Why do you allow your children to go train for the army? There is no country that has declared war on South Africa. Do you want your children to come and kill our children?"[270] Albertina was not oblivious to the fact that her action would earn her further trouble, but she believed in the struggle and attempted to impress it upon the White women that their silence over the atrocities committed by apartheid was morally questionable. Notably, although most White women did not speak out against apartheid as mentioned earlier, a number of them like Helen Joseph, Mary Benson, Paula Hathorn, Florence De Villiers, and the Black Sash members participated in the struggle.

Emma Mashinini

Emma Mashinini's anti-apartheid struggle was in the area of the workers union. Like the other women involved in the struggle, Emma received her ample share of reprisals from the authorities. She remembers that during one of her traumatic detention experiences, she saw her child's face but could not remember her name because her mind was totally blank.[271] Emma, like many Black women of her time, had little formal education or professional skills. However, she displayed a lot of common sense and dedication to the cause of her people. Gay W. Seidman describes Emma as follows.

---

269 Ibid.
270 Ibid.
271 Mashinini, "Life As a Trade-Union Leader" in Russell, *Lives of Courage*, 178.

> A leading figure in the black trade union movement and in the political struggle against apartheid, her persistent courage has been extraordinary. Having left junior high school to work first as a nanny and later as a textile worker, and while raising her children on her own, in 1975 she became the first national organizer for a fledgling union for black workers in the service sector.[272]

The historical significance of Emma's involvement in the struggle against apartheid lies in her ability to transcend class and gender biases. Emma experienced various manifestations of male domination at the hands of her employer, the security police. and prison supervisors. Prior to the beginning of her role as an advocate for poor Black workers, she had been divorced and become a single parent, saddled with the onerous responsibilities of raising her children alone under unusually difficult circumstances. There is no question about the importance of the sacrifice made by other women leaders in the effort to bring about social change in South Africa. But unlike Winnie and Albertina, Emma lacked the political background associated with being married to a prominent political activist. However, she liked working with people and was naturally an astute organizer and speaker who worked hard to bring poor Black workers together to fight for better working conditions and in the process, challenge the status quo.

As a staunch member of the Anglican Church, Emma effectively used the church as a forum to educate and encourage fellow Blacks to join the struggle for change by updating the Christian community on the conditions of political prisoners.[273] Her single motivation in joining the struggle was to be a voice for Black employees, who comprised almost "85 percent of South Africa's 36 million people not classified whites."[274] Emma held strong views concerning the role of the church on behalf of the victims of apartheid. For her, just as the workers' unions

---

272 Mashinini, *Strikes Have Followed Me All My Life*, xx.
273 Ibid.
274 Ibid., xxi.

were expected to stay engaged in the struggle for political and economic change "the church must also face the fact that it has to be involved in the political situation." Believing that "We are extremely lucky that the highest person in our church, Desmond Tutu, speaks out against injustices," she suggested that "priests must not stand in their pulpits and preach about the suffering of the people" because the Church "will suffer if it doesn't get involved."[275] Emma was able to draw many Blacks to her own side of the debate concerning the role of the church in the politics of apartheid South Africa. For them, the church could either practice what it preached by joining in the struggle or abdicate its moral authority by ignoring the voice of the oppressed.

In 1975, Emma started "a black shop-workers union," currently known as the Commercial Catering and Allied Workers' Union of South Africa or CCAWUSA. She worked as the general secretary of this organization from its inception through its emergence in the 1980s as the second-largest union in South Africa with a membership of over 70,000.[276] As CCAWUSA assumed the role of mouthpiece for Black workers in South Africa, Emma gained organizational experience through her association with some White and Colored union leaders. Her colleagues include Bobby Robarts, Morris Kagan, Alan Fine, and Ray Altman, leaders of the National Union of Commercial and Allied Workers (NUCAW) and the National Union of Distributive Workers (NUDW). These two unions represented Colored and Indian shop workers.[277] Mashinini was mostly inspired by Roberts, a dynamic and eloquent woman. She decided to take on the challenge. However, Kagan and Fine were also helpful.[278] Accordingly, Mashinini acknowledged that Kagan, a member of the White-only trade union, "helped her a lot in the formation of the union."[279] The support Emma received from White trade unionists is indicative of the fact that among every human

---

275 Russell, *Lives of Courage*, 179.
276 Ibid; Helene Perold, *Working Women: A Portrait of South Africa's Black Women Workers* (Johannesburg: Ravan Press (Pty.) Ltd. 1985), 30.
277 Mashinini, *Strikes Have Followed Me All My Life*, 31–33.
278 Ibid., 31.
279 Mashinini, in Russell, *Lives of Courage*, 182.

group or race, there are always certain individuals who are willing to cross traditional boundaries and take a stance against injustice, even at the cost of being ostracized by members of their group.

Emma was aware of the fact that some union leaders had been detained or forced into exile because of their opposition to apartheid. But she insisted on creating a grassroots union for Black workers. Due to the Group Areas Act, which forbade such organizational efforts by Blacks and other opponents of the system, she could not secure office space in the White area of Johannesburg. She managed to secure rooms in Princess House, which was located in the center of the city.[280] After obtaining office space, she had to contend with the challenges of obtaining funds and finding members for the new union.[281] To find members, she had to reach out to Black workers by word of mouth, paying visits to the workers at their homes and workplaces, and distributing leaflets. In the process, she inevitably got in the employers' black books, and this was the beginning of her confrontations with apartheid.[282]

Emma's union collaborated with other unions whose leaders believed in the common struggle for justice. They embarked on projects like writing letters on behalf of their unions, which were published in *Rand Daily Mail*, a liberal paper that was later closed by the apartheid regime. They organized strikes to force the employers to the bargaining table, such as the so-called red meat boycott and fought in the streets on behalf of their members.[283] Notably, every act of protest was carried out for a specific cause, which in turn helped to expose the contradiction of apartheid rule. For example, the red meat boycott was aimed at seeking redress on behalf of abattoir workers in the Western Cape who were unfairly dismissed by their White employers.[284] Acting on information from these employers, apartheid police agents harassed, arrested, and

---

280 Mashinini, *Strikes Have Followed Me All My Life*, 31; Mashinini's interview in *Working Women*, 130–133.
281 Mashinini, *Strikes Have Followed Me All My Life*, 32.
282 Ibid., 34–35.
283 Ibid., 46–48.
284 Ibid. 46.

detained Emma on a regular basis. Ultimately, Emma's experience demonstrates the fact that apartheid was an elaborate network of landlords, employers, and state agents who were predominantly White males, linked by their common commitment to the preservation of their political and economic dominance.[285]

She was frequently arrested and detained for her union activities. For example, in November 1981 she was detained in solitary confinement for six months. Some other trade union leaders were also arrested and detained around the same time.[286] Such arrests and detentions were made under the General Laws Amendment Act and Section 22, which was part of the Terrorist Act, "which permitted police to hold people for fourteen days without charge."[287] Or Section 6, which required solitary confinement.[288] Invariably, detentions under apartheid laws involved physical and psychological torture for the victims.[289] Like many detainees, Neil Aggett, a White medical doctor who was helping Black trade unionists, died at the hands of his captors.[290]

Emma and her family were also involved in the Detainees Parents' Support Committee.[291] Emma's husband, Tom, was among the first people to get involved because of his experience with unfair detention, trial, and torture at the hands of the racist regime. Max and Audrey Coleman, committed White anti-apartheid activists whose son was in detention, were also active members of this important support group.[292] The DPSC was responsible for organizing the "Free the Children" campaign, both in South Africa and around the world. Because of the courageous work of groups such as this, detainees got some attention from the international press, the diplomatic community, and foreign

---

285 Ibid., 75.
286 Russell, *Lives of Courage,* 179.
287 Mashinini, *Strikes Have Followed Me All My Life,* 47.
288 Ibid., 62.
289 Ibid., 63, 69–70; Russell, *Lives of Courage,* 9, 12, 15, 24.
290 Ibid., 54–55; Ibid., 185.
291 Russell, *Lives of Courage,* 180.
292 Ibid., 81.

investors.²⁹³ The resulting publicity made the apartheid government very uncomfortable as its intimidations, harassments, threats, and similar terrorist tactics were being exposed to the global community.

In 1985, Emma was involved in the formation of the Congress of South African Trade Unions (COSATU).²⁹⁴ Following successful negotiations with the management, Black workers were able to secure an annual salary increase. More importantly, as Emma states, "we were the first union in South Africa — black, white, or Coloured — to have an agreement that protects women's maternity rights. It does not extend to women being paid during their maternity leave, except for what is required by law, but women cannot now lose their jobs or be demoted because of pregnancy."²⁹⁵

A Black woman with little education, Emma clearly earned herself a place in history as a powerful spokesperson for South Africa's Black workers. By catering to the interests of one of the most vulnerable groups in South Africa in the course of her involvement in the workers' union, she became a figure to reckon with in the struggle against apartheid.

Emma also acknowledged that women's involvement in the struggle against apartheid should also encourage them to liberate themselves from internalized sexism. As a confident Black woman, she saw some problems with the fact that many women accepted the position of the "inferior" sex or group in society. She just could not understand this and wished that women could liberate themselves from this situation. For example, during an interview in January 1985, she said that

> up until a year ago there were equal numbers of men and women on our executive (six men, six women). But we had our elections and now there are eight men and four women. But who's responsible for that? It's the women themselves. I don't know why. It's the women who will always elect a man. Why? What deceives them?

---

293 Ibid.
294 Mashinini in Russell, 188.
295 Ibid., 187; Mashinini's interview in Perold, *Working Women*, 132.

Because when we are in meetings the women are more outspoken than men. And with the strikes, you find that the people who've always actually worked very hard to see that the strike comes into being – it's the women. And for the strike to be a success – it's the women. And when it's negotiated and it's time to go back to work, or whatever – the people who opt for it are the women. Women are at the forefront of everything . . . and the men co-operate.[296]

Thenjiwe Mtintso

Thenjiwe Mtintso, popularly known as "Thenjie," was born in 1950 in Soweto. According to June Goodwin in *Cry Amandla: South African Women and the Question of Power,* she became politically conscious of apartheid at age twenty-three when she joined the South African Student Organization (SASO) at Fort Hare University, where she was a medical student.[297] She is described as "a political organizer, a street fighter, in training full time to dismantle apartheid."[298] She helped organize student strikes in 1972 and 1973 respectively. During the 1972 strike, the students wanted to establish a representative council in all the universities to address their grievances. Commenting on the ensuing demonstrations, Thenjiwe describes how she and her colleagues would "walk in the street and not move apart as whites approached. They got real scared, which amused us, and we would tell them we were *swart gevaar* — Afrikaans for 'black peril.' I interpret it as perhaps a childish stage, but it can be traced to anger."[299] The 1973 strike lasted for a month, after which Thenjie was dismissed from college because of her political activities.[300]

---

296 Mashinini's interview in Working Women, 130–131.
297 Goodwin, *Cry Amandla*, 19.
298 Ibid., 4.
299 Ibid., 19.
300 Ibid., 19–20.

Thenjiwe and her fellow students persuaded their parents to support their cause, arguing that the struggle against apartheid should be extended to the local communities. Toward this end, she embarked on "speaking tours" along with other students to explain their position, and she was a good speaker. It was during this period that she met Steve Biko, also a dismissed medical student and the leader of the Black Consciousness Movement.[301] Biko had a tremendous impact on Thenjie's political life. He had put together some programs for King William's Town, which became the Black Nationalist Center.[302] Thenjie joined this community in 1974 and became a full-time anti-apartheid activist.[303] The Black Consciousness ideals were modeled after Marcus Mosiah Garvey's ideals of Black pride. In 1977, the movement was banned.[304]

Having been forced to abandon her medical training and the opportunities that went with it, Thenjie was not afraid of the consequences of confronting the apartheid system. Although she had already tasted the cruelty associated with being a detainee through the apartheid security agents, she refused to answer questions by the latter that were aimed at implicating Biko. During one of her detentions when the agents were interrogating her, she refused to admit that Steve had arranged for some people to leave South Africa for military training.[305] She further refused to sign an incriminating statement under duress. As a result, she was beaten and dehumanized while being transferred from one prison to another by her captors (she was detained, interrogated, beaten, and starved in Kingstown prison, East London prison, Umtata prison, Ngqamakwe prison, and then Nqanduli prison). Even when she

---

301 Winnie Mandela, *Part of My Soul*, 121; Nelson Mandela, *Long Walk to Freedom*, 486–488; Russell, *Lives of Courage*, 9.
302 Goodman, *Cry Amandla*, 20–21; Thenjiwe Mtintson, speaking to UNESCO radio, September 1980 in Perold, *Working Women*, 28–29.
303 Ibid., 21.
304 Ibid., 169; Themjiwe Mtintso, speaking to UNESCO radio, September 1980 in Perold, *Working Women*, 28.
305 Goodman, *Cry Amandla*, 170.

was thrown into a cell infested with lice and bees, and hung like a cloth, she still refused to sign the statement.³⁰⁶

Thenjie also carried out her protest against apartheid by frequently refusing to ride in the police car when she was ordered to appear in court. She would tell the police that she would drive herself to court, and she maintained that the police were not legally authorized to order people to appear in court.³⁰⁷ For instance, on January 15, 1979, when the police phoned her and ordered her to be picked up the next day for a court appearance, she responded that only a magistrate had the power to order people to appear in court and not the police. She further argued that she was going to drive herself to court, and that court opened at 9:00 AM instead of 6:30 AM as wrongfully specified by the police.³⁰⁸ A single parent who juggled her responsibilities toward her family and community, Thenjiwe refused to succumb to every machination devised by the security agents to break her spirit. She remained a very brave woman and successfully eluded her tormentors by escaping from the country on a number of occasions. Interestingly, her occasional disappearances helped expose the contradictions of apartheid rule as they usually made interesting headlines.³⁰⁹ Whenever Thenjie traveled to neighboring countries like Lesotho and Botswana, the authorities became very uncomfortable because she would share critical information about the home front with the international press as well as friends and colleagues in the struggle.³¹⁰

Sometimes, when a leader dies his or her disciples feel discouraged, and some even decide to abandon their cause. As an ardent follower of Steve Biko, Thenjie continued to carry on the struggle even after the untimely death of her mentor on September 11, 1977, in the hands of the apartheid police.³¹¹ She would later on a switch from the Black

---

306 Ibid., 170–178.
307 Ibid., 181.
308 Ibid.
309 Ibid., 182.
310 Ibid., 172, 185.
311 Ibid., 11, 185.

Consciousness Movement to the ANC,[312] as Goodwin states, "not for sentimental reasons, but for deeply felt political reasons."[313] As Thenjie's friend Reebs Musi explains,

> After Steve's death, things didn't really come to a stop. We always felt at some stage or other one of us is going to die and it doesn't mean the end of the world. There is this belief among black people that when one dies, he lives with you spiritually, a sort of god with a small "g." Those who are dead know and see whatever you do. Wherever Steve is, he wouldn't be happy if we stopped. He would be happy to see us going on and on and on.[314]

Thenjie's political activities eventually sent her to Lesotho as a refugee, with a single mission in mind: to survey the refugees.[315] She left her son, Lumumba, with her mother in Soweto. She thought that life in exile would be too hard for a child. Upon her arrival in Lesotho, she was warmly received by exiled members of the Black Consciousness Movement who were already there.[316] Initially life was boring in exile, but she understood quite well that it was time for her to settle abroad and extend her services to the refugee community. While in Lesotho, Thenjie continued to be a very outspoken and thoughtful leader, especially among Blacks. For example, she tried to encourage members of the ANC and the Pan African Congress to get together and resolve their differences.[317] She did not approve of the fact that the two groups had placed negative "labels" on each other on account of their ideological differences. ANC members called PAC members "capitalists," while PAC members called ANC members "communists." Also, PAC

---

312 Ibid., 186.
313 Ibid., 188.
314 Ibid., 185.
315 Ibid., 189; Themjiwe Mtintso, speaking to UNESCO radio, September 1980 in Perold, *Working Women*, 28.
316 Goodman, *Cry Amandla*, 188.
317 Ibid., 193.

members did not accept the idea that South Africa belonged to all that live in it regardless of their racial backgrounds—an idea contained in the ANC's Freedom Charter of 1955. For the same reason, the ANC was criticized by the PAC leadership for being an inclusive organization.[318] Perhaps Winnie Mandela presented the most compelling argument for ANC's philosophy in the following statement.

> The ANC is committed to non-racialism. . . . The umbrella organization of the ANC embodies everyone who is fighting side by side with us against oppression . . . The South Africa of tomorrow that I'm fighting for will include that white child who has been so brave defying his Broederbond parents and shouting the slogans of my movement on the campus. I can't ignore him. He is part of us.[319]

Given her decision to join the ANC and subsequently mediate the differences between the PAC and the ANC, it is evident that Thenjiwe was not opposed to Winnie's vision of the struggle. But she also subscribed to the ideology of Black nationalism espoused by Biko's Black Consciousness Movement, which she regarded as a necessary tool for the mobilization of Blacks against apartheid. From the standpoint of her earlier organization, the goal of the struggle was to address the issues of race, nationalism, class, and capitalism. She clarified her position by saying that "In South Africa, a rural person understands mainly racial oppression and not any class analysis. People will mobilize first around nationalism. Black Consciousness deals very well with the national question; its ideology of black pride cannot be banned."[320] Thenjie took the message of Black pride to heart because of the crisis the apartheid regime created in South Africa. For Blacks, this crisis was especially manifested in the form of extreme poverty, starvation, and lack of basic

---

318 Ibid., 192-194.
319 Winnie Mandela, *Part of My Soul*, 120.
320 Goodman, *Cry Amandla*, 194–195.

human rights. She compared the death of Steve Biko to that of Christ because in her view both leaders gave their lives for justice for all. In her own words, Steve "fought for the kind of justice Christ stood for."[321] Thenjie, a nonviolent woman by nature, eventually embraced the idea of an armed struggle against apartheid. In what appeared to reflect her political maturation, she was converted to the idea that apartheid did not understand the language of peace because it is inherently a violent system. Therefore, it was more inclined to enter into a dialogue only when it has been confronted with credible force. On account of her ideological conversion, Thenjiwe was determined to undergo military training, but the arthritis in her leg prevented her.[322]

Conclusion

Black women's contributions to the struggle against apartheid were an aggregate of the efforts of individuals who strove to bring about changes on both the personal and group levels. While focusing on this collective struggle, this chapter has highlighted the activities of a selected number of Black women leaders who served as an inspiration for not only their fellow women but men as well. These are representative actors whose personal stories mirror the pain, frustration, determination, and aspirations of their colleagues and fellow victims of apartheid. Besides carrying their fair share of the burden of the struggle, these women served as spokespersons on behalf of their families, friends, fellow women, and the country. With many Black male leaders imprisoned, exiled, or murdered, they embraced the challenge of leadership. Winnie spoke on behalf of these heroines of the anti-apartheid movement when she said the following about her frustration relative to the ruthlessness of the White minority regime.

---

321 Ibid., 191.
322 Ibid., 196–197.

> Talking of "change" in this country: I was in prison for the first time in 1958, my first pregnancy was there. And I was visited by my children in that same prison eighteen years later in 1976 - the very daughter that I had been expecting when I was in that prison for the first time, in pursuit of the very same ideals.[323]

Like Winnie, each of these women leaders was inspired by the brutality of apartheid to do more for her country instead of being discouraged.

Like their leaders discussed in this chapter, Black women's contributions toward the effort to dismantle apartheid derived in part from their ability to forge credible alliances with other groups and non-Black women. In *Women and Resistance in South Africa*, Cherryl Walker writes about the Federation of South African Women (FSAW), the first and most inclusive women's anti-apartheid organization, which was active from 1954 through 1963. The FSAW organized demonstrations or conferences in 1954, 1956, and 1958, in Johannesburg and Pretoria respectively, against the extension of passes to Black women.[324] The majority of the delegates were indigenous African women.[325] Women from other ethnic and racial backgrounds were involved, both with the planning and demonstrations. A major historical development related to the 1954 conference was the "Women's Charter" contained in the "final report on the conference."[326] Equally significant was the attendees' decision to adopt "specific aims for the new organization" summarized as follows: universal suffrage; equal employment, equal pay, and equal promotion opportunities; equal rights with men; equal educational opportunities, good health care, day care, affordable housing, water, sanitation, light, transport, modern amenities for South Africans.[327]

---

323 Winnie Mandela, *Part of My Soul*, 118.
324 Cherryl Walker, *Women and Resistance in South Africa* (London: Onyx Press Ltd. 1982), 153–164.
325 Ibid. 161.
326 Ibid., 153.
327 Ibid., 159.

Most of the above issues reflect the special interests and concerns of the women as pillars of both their families and the communities during the apartheid era. They also wanted unrestricted freedom of political expression, women's participation in other organizations like trade unions, and collaboration with other organizations that shared similar ideals in South Africa and around the world.[328] As a matter of fact, the following year, 1955, the ANC's Freedom Charter expanded on these women's ideals. At the August 9, 1956, anti-pass demonstration, the women argued that the pass laws were the most cruel of all the apartheid laws because it made the Africans prisoners. They dumped thousands of signatures at Prime Minister J. G. Strydom's[329] office door and declared war on apartheid by saying, "You have tampered with the women, you have struck a rock."[330] Notably, when the prime minister saw about twenty thousand angry women gathered around the Unions Building in Pretoria, he ran away for his safety.[331] Evidently, he had underestimated the determination of these women to fight for their rights.

Lastly, the women combined their struggle for equal political and economic opportunities with their struggle against sexism at both the local and national levels. Black women realized that in spite of the fact that they and their male relatives shared a common experience relative to racial oppression under apartheid, and in spite of their proven determination to join the men in the struggle against their common oppressors, they were still not treated as equals by their male counterparts. As the report on women's activities elaborates,

> Many men who are politically active and progressive in outlook still follow the tradition that women should take no part in politics and a great resentment exists towards women who seek independent activities or even express independent opinions. This prejudice is so strong that

---

328 Ibid.
329 Ibid., 181.
330 Ibid., 189, 195.
331 Ibid., 195.

even when many of those in leadership positions in the ANC appear to be co-operating with the Federation, it is sometimes difficult to avoid the conclusion that they would prefer to hinder the work of the Federation and to withdraw their womenfolk from activities.[332]

For Black women, the anti-apartheid struggle provided an opportunity to emancipate themselves from multiple forms of oppression. As they declared,

> As members of the National Liberation movements and Trade Unions . . . we march forward with our men in the struggle for liberation and the defense of the working people . . . As women there rests upon us also the burden of removing from our society all the social differences developed in past times between men and women which have the effect of keeping our sex in a position of inferiority and subordination.[333]

As mentioned earlier, Black women were determined to share equal political, economic, and social powers with men.[334] This issue of power-sharing in post-apartheid South Africa that the women had fought very hard for during the anti-apartheid struggle will be discussed in detail in the next chapter.

---

332 Ibid., 196.
333 Ibid., 156.
334 Russell, *Lives of Courage*, 129–132, 195–199.

CHAPTER 5

Conclusion: Black Women In Post-Apartheid South Africa

The victory of this struggle against apartheid is the absolute condition for any change in the social status of the women as a whole; their participation is an expression not only of their desire to rid South Africa of the curse of apartheid, but also of their deep concern for their own status as women[335]

—Hilda Bernstein

It is vitally important that all the structures of Government, including the President should understand fully that freedom cannot be achieved unless women have been emancipated from all forms of oppression[336]

—President Nelson Mandela

---

335 Hilda Bernstein, *For Their Triumphs and for their Tears: Conditions and Resistance of Women in* Apartheid *South Africa* (International Defence & Aid Fund, August 1975), 60.
336 President Nelson Mandela, opening South Africa's first democratically elected parliament on 24 May 1994, in *Gender Matters*, Quarterly by the Commission on Gender Equality, Vol. 1 (October–December 2000), 4.

The duty to transform our country to achieve gender equality for all is our responsibility — all of us[337]

—Chairperson, Center for Gender Equality

Introduction

IN THE PRECEDING chapters of this work, we have examined the status of Black women in precolonial South Africa, their conditions under colonial rule and apartheid rule, and their contributions to the struggle against White minority rule. The final chapter begins with an overview of the interplay of domestic and international factors that contributed to the eventual collapse of apartheid. As suggested by Nelson Mandela in the second passage quoted above, one way of measuring the outcome of the anti-apartheid struggle is by looking at the condition of women, especially Black women, in post-apartheid South Africa. Obviously, given the fact that South Africa made the transition from a White minority dictatorship to multiracial democracy only in 1994, it is premature to assess the full impact of the new political dispensation on the status of Black women. Yet it is logical to expect that South Africa's first democratic constitution would be a fairly reliable indicator of the government's commitment to gender equality. As the highest law in the land, the federal constitution should protect the rights of all South Africans regardless of their gender, race, or class. Therefore, this chapter is centrally concerned with the provisions, if any, contained in the new constitution that are designed to empower women by assuring them meaningful participation in the political, social, and economic aspects of national life in post-apartheid South Africa.

---

337 CGE chairperson at the launch of the Gender, Advertising and Broadcasting Report, CGE Symposium, 2000 1994, in *Gender Matters*, 4.

From Apartheid to Multiracial Democracy

As discussed in chapter 3, if Sharpeville and Soweto epitomized the centrality of violence as the instrument by which the White racial hegemony was safeguarded in apartheid South Africa, they also reflected the growing crisis of legitimacy that confronted Pretoria during the last three decades preceding the collapse of apartheid. For instance, following the Soweto shootings in 1976, Black schoolchildren, for the first time, rejected Afrikaans as the language of instruction in the schools on grounds that it was a colonial language. Not only did Black parents condemn the killings, mass arrests, detentions, torture, and interrogations of their children by security agents, they vowed to support their cause. Specifically, Black women became increasingly adamant in their determination to dismantle the racist system (see chapter 3). With political instability came economic instability as riots and protests became the order of the day in South Africa. And in the next couple of years, there were clear signs that apartheid was crumbling.

According to an Igbo proverb, "He who is holding another person down is holding himself down as well." To the extent that the apartheid regime maintained its iron grip on the necks of its victims, there were some costs to whites as well, and over the years, the use of violent tactics to suppress the demands for racial justice became counterproductive. As Leonard Thompson states, "By 1978, the apartheid state was in trouble. South Africa's economic boom of the 1960s and early 1970s had been followed by a sharp recession. The administration of the complex network of apartheid laws was proving to be extremely costly."[338] Moreover, by 1977 Whites were leaving South Africa in large numbers as murder, rape, assault, and other forms of crimes had reached a climax. This situation helped to erode the power base of the apartheid regime as both the private and public sectors of the economy were experiencing a significant shortage of skilled labor.[339]

---

338 Leonard Thompson, *A History of South Africa* (New Haven: Yale University Press, 1995), 221.
339 Ibid.

In addition, there were demographic trends that were turning the table on apartheid in significant ways as the White population declined from roughly 21 percent of the total population in the 1970s to 16 percent in the 1980s, and to 10 percent in the 1990s.[340] At the same time, as conditions in the homelands continued to deteriorate, Blacks migrated to the cities in large numbers, with some living in shacks without good water and electricity.[341] The new migrants defied the influx control efforts of the government, the pass laws, the Urban Areas Act, and similar measures. Interestingly, despite the harsh conditions under which they were forced to live under the apartheid system, Blacks gradually emerged as a potent economic force as their purchasing power grew over the years. This development was possible as a result of their large population and their determination to survive under very harsh conditions. By 1985, Blacks had about 31.8 percent of disposable income (income from all sources after taxation), Whites 55 percent, Coloreds 8.8 percent, and Indians 3.9 percent. By the late 1980s, many Blacks (as well as Colored and Indians) were reaching the middle level of employment in the industrial sector, and some had reached the managerial level.[342]

Educational achievement played a critical part in the growth of Black purchasing power during the decades of apartheid. Although the White minority government maintained its policy of separate and inferior education for Blacks, and although the Bantu education system faced frequent disruption as a result of strikes and boycotts, Blacks managed to make significant gains in education over the years. For instance, in 1986 there were more than 7,000,000 Black schoolchildren (including 6,000,000 Africans) in South Africa, and fewer than 1,000,000 Whites. In the senior classes (equivalent to the eleventh and twelfth grades in the United States), there were three times as many Blacks (including 2.5 times as many Africans) as Whites. At the same time, the number

---

340 Ibid., 222, 241.
341 Ibid., 241.
342 Ibid., 242.

of Black university students was approaching parity with Whites.[343] Another implication was that Africans would be graduating from school in larger numbers than European children, and their purchasing power would only continue to grow. Also, educated Africans would be employed at managerial and supervisory positions, and eventually make up the majority of senior-level workers in the economy.

During the 1980s, the South African economy continued to deteriorate as Whites, who controlled middle and upper-level employment, did not always have the needed education and skills. Thus, inefficiency and poor service delivery became common features of South Africa's economic system. At this time, South African goods were too expensive in the overseas markets because workers' wages had gone up due to the efforts of the trade unions (see chapter 4), and could not compete favorably with products from other parts of the world, especially Asia, Latin America, and Eastern Europe.[344]

In addition to these internal factors, international sanctions were having a negative effect on the South African economy in the 1980s. In the United States, an anti-apartheid protest coordinated by Randall Robinson of Trans-Africa attracted clergy, students, trade unionists, and civil rights leaders.[345] International dignitaries made trips to Southern Africa to hold talks with both the government and opposition groups, especially ANC leaders in Robben Island and in exile. Anti-apartheid sentiments had also grown strong in Australia, where trade unions showed strong support for their South African counterparts. For example, Emma Mashinini reports that trade unions in Australia refused to unload South African goods upon hearing about Neil Aggett's death while in solitary confinement because of his involvement in union activities. In February 1986, the Australian trade unions prevented the South African multinationals from opening a Pick 'n' Pay branch or supermarket in Melbourne. The following month, the Commonwealth Eminent Persons Group (EPG) visited South Africa on

---

343 Ibid.
344 Thompson, *History of South Africa*, 242.
345 Ibid., 233.

a fact-finding mission. Emma Mashinini was invited to a meeting with them because of her involvement in both the trade unions and Women Against Apartheid. The group was allowed access to influential Black political figures like Nelson Mandela. It is of historical significance that Mashinini was invited to this important meeting because neither the government nor the male-dominated opposition cared very much to invite Black women to such negotiations. The publication of the EPG report in the same year amidst the growing international outcry for the abolition of apartheid increased the pressure on the White minority regime.[346]

As a result of the anti-apartheid movement in the United States and Europe, foreign investors began to withdraw from or minimize their presence in South Africa in the 1980s. For instance, following the 1985 decision by Chase Manhattan bank not to "roll over its short-term loans," other banks followed their lead, and the South African economy suffered serious financial crises.[347] According to the World Bank, South Africa was in deep trouble by 1987, with inflation at roughly 15 percent between 1980 and 1987. In the late 1980s, it had the third worst economy among industrialized countries, only better than Turkey and Israel. The South African Reserve Bank testified to the country's growing economic troubles when it announced in 1988 that "In the present international political climate the capital account remains the Achilles heel of South Africa's balance of payments."[348]

It is not surprising that the 1980s witnessed the first serious effort by the Botha government to initiate some "reforms" as apartheid had clearly proven to be an inefficient and expensive system in the midst of an economic recession. With three parliamentary chambers; fourteen departments of education, health, and welfare; a big military and police establishment; and Black homelands that were unable to support themselves financially, the system had become unwieldy, especially in

---

346 Emma Mashinini, *Strikes Have Followed Me All My Life: A South African Autobiography* (New York: Routledge, 1991), 119–120.
347 Ibid., 233.
348 Ibid., 243.

view of government policy of segregation in every aspect of national life. According to some keen observers of apartheid, during one of his public speeches, Prime Minister Botha acknowledged that apartheid was no longer useful and that the system should be changed to include Africans in the decision-making process in South Africa.[349]

However, although the prime minister acknowledged the contradictions of apartheid, he was inclined to pursue cosmetic reforms that included the creation of a separate parliament for the Asians and the Colored and none for the Africans, and his decision in 1986 to repeal the pass laws, Natives Land Act, and Group Areas Act. Botha's reforms also included the so-called orderly urbanization policy and the creation of so-called multiracial councils in the metropolitan regions.[350] Notably, Botha's new urban policy was a bogus promise as it was designed to segregate urban populations in zones, with the Africans living in the most depressed parts of the cities, without jobs, good and adequate housing, and other amenities. Furthermore, this concession was only to Africans residing outside the so-called independent homelands such as Venda, Ciskei, Transkei, and Bophuthatswana. Similarly, the government decided to divide South Africa into four metropolitan regions: Port Elizabeth, Durban-Pinetown, Cape Town, and Pretoria-Witwatersrand-Vereeniging triangle. Although it was decided that each region would have a multiracial council, which would have included the Africans, council members would be appointed by the government. Finally, a new executive committee established by the Botha administration to oversee general affairs was to be appointed, as opposed to being democratically elected, with Africans excluded as well.[351]

For Black women and other anti-apartheid groups, these "reforms" were not enough. These groups rejected both the regional councils and executive committees on grounds that they were undemocratic. Clearly, the above arrangements would not have been in the interest of Black people. Moreover, segregation remained in effect in critical sectors of

---

349 From Race Relations Survey, 1986, in Thompson, *History of South Africa*, 227.
350 Thompson, *History of South Africa*, 226–227.
351 Ibid.

society with a persistent gap in the funding of White schools and Black schools, as well as health and social services delivered to Whites and Blacks. Government classification of popular constituencies continued along racial lines, and Whites continued to be disproportionately over-represented in government under the new constitution. Africans still could not own lands outside the reserves. The government continued to force African families out of their homes, and squatter camps continued to be destroyed, especially on the outskirts of major cities like Port Elizabeth and Cape Town.[352] To add salt to injury, talks about including Africans in the decision-making process were only "empty talks." Black people were still being arrested and placed in solitary confinement without trial and without informing their families, friends, and lawyers. Africans continued to be incarcerated and executed in alarming numbers. Mashinini states that between 1988 and 1989, the criminal justice system imposed 213 death sentences on Africans, with 117 executed, 48 reprieved, and only 27 successful appeals. Blacks were executed seven at a time, and their families were not allowed to see their bodies.[353] Most important of all, the government continued to reject demands for equal participation in government by Africans, who made up about 75 percent of the national population.[354]

In retrospect, it appears that the Botha regime was buying time in order to prepare South Africa for what it must have perceived as the impending fall of a system that, for decades, was instrumental to the preservation of White privilege in the political, economic, and social spheres. The political ascendency of a more liberal wing of the White ruling class with the election of President De Klerk in late 1989 sealed the fate of the apartheid system. Although he was a loyal member of the National Party, De Klerk, like many Afrikaners of his generation, understood that apartheid faced a certain doom in the face of mounting domestic and international pressure. He reasoned that the best hope for the White community was to negotiate a settlement from a position of

---

352 Ibid.
353 Mashinini, *Strikes Have Followed Me* All My Life, 133.
354 Thompson, *History of South Africa*, 225–228.

strength. On February 11, 1990, Nelson Mandela was released from prison after twenty-seven years of incarceration. Subsequently, the transition from apartheid to multiracial democracy proceeded rapidly, and in April 1994 Mandela became the first democratically elected president of South Africa.[355]

Black Women and the 1996 Constitution

As a result of the shortcomings of the 1984 constitution, the mounting domestic and international pressures for reform, and the eventual collapse of apartheid in 1994, a new democratic constitution was needed to serve as a legal foundation for post-apartheid society.[356] As stated earlier in this chapter, although it may be premature to assess the impact of the post-apartheid system on South African women, the 1996 constitution should at least contain provisions that ensure an opportunity for representation in the new dispensation. In many ways, this constitution is different from the 1984 constitution. First, it reflects the rich and diverse heritage and ideals of all South African peoples. Second, it expands on the ideals of the Freedom Charter established by FSAW in 1954 and ANC's Freedom Charter of 1955. Each of the two documents was designed by the founding organization as a blueprint for a democratic South Africa (see chapter 4). Third, the 1996 constitution represents the collective creation of the people of South Africa, because representative individuals and groups participated in the process that eventually produced it. As a matter of fact, the South African constitution is widely regarded as one of the most democratic constitutions in the world. From the standpoint of South African women and other groups, translating the ideals represented in the new constitution into reality is perhaps the next big hurdle for this fragile democracy. There are clear provisions for gender equality as well as the equality of all South Africans before the law. In the final analysis, Black women's struggle

---

355 Ibid., pp. 241–254.
356 Ibid., 225.

against apartheid has earned all South African women a place in their country's constitution. In this respect, the preamble is noteworthy:

> We, the people of South Africa, Recognise the injustices of our past; Honor those who suffered for justice and freedom in our land; Respect those who have worked to build and develop our country; and Believe that South Africa belongs to all who live in it, united in our diversity. We therefore, through our freely elected representatives, adopt this Constitution as the supreme law of the Republic so as to heal the divisions of the past and establish a society based on democratic values, social justice and fundamental human rights; Lay the foundations for a democratic and open society in which government is based on the will of the people and every citizen is equally protected by law; Improve the quality of life of all citizens and free the potential of each person; and Build a united and democratic South Africa able to take its rightful place as a sovereign state in the family of nations. May God protect our people. Nkosi Sikelel' iAfrika. Morena boloka setjhaba sa heso. God seen Suid-Africa. God bless South Africa. Mudzimu fhatutshedza Afurika. Hosi katekisa Africa.[357]

As discussed in chapters 1 and 2, apartheid was predicated on the negative ideals of racism, sexism, and classicism. Black women wanted South Africa to address the issues of race, gender, and class, and the new constitution contains provisions for legal safeguards against all manner of discrimination. As stated in chapter 2, under the apartheid system, Black women continued to be denied some of the political, social, and economic rights and privileges that were available to Black men in pre-apartheid South Africa. In theory, Black women have broken

---

357 Constitution of the Republic of South Africa, Preamble, http://www.polity.org.za/govdocs/constitution/saconst.html.

those racial and gender barriers that they had to endure in precolonial South Africa and colonial/apartheid South Africa. The new constitution promises to undo those barriers when it states that there should be "Non-racialism and Non-sexism in the Republic of South Africa."[358]

The framers of the 1996 constitution chose words carefully in an effort to faithfully represent the egalitarian and inclusive spirit of the constitution. For instance, in Chapter 1/Schedule 3: Section 3:2:b, gender-neutral terms like "Chairperson" and "Deputy Chairperson" are used in regard to the composition of the National Council of Provinces in order to reassure women that they would have a place in the new dispensation. In the past, masculine terms would have dominated the language of the constitution; this would have been normal since key political positions were typically occupied by men.[359]

Chapter 2 of the constitution discusses the Bill of Rights. Since this work focuses on women, it is pertinent to focus on the theme of "equality" in Section 7, Subsections 9:1, 2, 3, 4, 5. Here, the constitution states that

> everyone is equal before the law and has the right to equal protection and benefit of the law. Equality includes the full and equal enjoyment of all rights and freedoms. To promote the achievement of equality, legislative and other measures designed to protect or advance persons, or categories of persons, disadvantaged by unfair discrimination may be taken. The state may not unfairly discriminate directly or indirectly against anyone on one or more grounds, including race, gender, sex, pregnancy, marital status, ethnic or social origin, colour, sexual orientation, age, disability, religion, conscience, belief, culture, language and birth. No person may unfairly discriminate directly or indirectly against anyone on one or more grounds in terms of subsection (3). National

---

358 Ibid., Founding Provisions, Chapter 1, Section 1, Subsection b.
359 Ibid., Election Procedures, Chapter 1, Schedule 3, Section 3, Subsection 2 b.

legislation must be enacted to prevent or prohibit unfair discrimination. Discrimination on one or more grounds listed in subsection (3) is unfair unless it is established that the discrimination is fair.[360]

On a related theme, the constitution states that "there is a common citizenship. All citizens are equally entitled to the rights, privileges and benefits of citizenship; and equally subject to the duties and responsibilities of citizenship. National legislation must provide for the acquisition, loss and restoration of citizenship."[361] Eventually, every South African is a full citizen by law, with all the privileges, benefits, and responsibilities. By implication, Black women have become full citizens of South Africa as well. The constitution empowers all women to make decisions about reproduction about the use of their bodies, and about medical or scientific experiments that could have important implications for women.[362] In other words, Black women can expect to be treated with respect and as adults. They will not be subjected to the searing pain of White paternalism discussed in chapter 3. Section 14 addresses the issue of personal privacy, which was a major concern for Black women, whose homes and personhood was frequently violated by agents of the apartheid regime.[363]

In recognition of Black women's struggle to ensure a better life for their children, Chapter 1, Sections 28, Subsections 1, 2, and 3 of the constitution states that all South African children—that is, people under the age of eighteen—are entitled to family care, basic nutrition, shelter, health care services, social services, basic education, and would not be subject to detention except in extreme circumstances. Finally, the hope and aspirations of Black mothers concerning basic and quality education for their children could become a reality.[364]

---

360 Ibid., Chapter 2, Section 7, Subsection 9: 1–5.
361 Ibid., Chapter 1, Section 3, Subsections 1, 2, 3.
362 Ibid., Chapter 1, Section 12, Subsection 2 (a, b, c).
363 Ibid., Chapter 1, Section 14, Subsection, a–d.
364 Ibid., Chapter 1, Section 28, Subsections 1–3; Chapter 2, Section 29, Subsections 1–4.

Conclusion

In 1997, the Commission on Gender Equality (CGE) was created in response to the mandate of the 1996 Constitution, which states that South Africa should promote and protect gender equality.[365] The CGE aims to turn this mandate into reality by adopting and promoting three principles in the public sphere: the principle of openness, the principle of transparency, and the principle of accountability.[366] The stated vision of CGE is to help South Africa create a society that is free from all forms of discrimination and oppression based on gender, race, class, religion, sexual orientation, disability, or geographic location. Its mission is to help bring about positive changes in South Africa by exposing "gender discrimination in laws, policies and practices; advocating changes in sexist attitudes and gender stereotypes; and instilling respect for women's rights as human rights."[367] CGE believes that "Women's emancipation is fundamental to the achievement of both gender equality and true democracy."[368] While it is interested in the welfare of all South Africans, it devotes special attention to highly marginalized groups, which include women in rural areas, on farms, in peri-urban areas, and in domestic employments.[369]

Given its autonomous status, the CGE should be expected to have the most accurate assessment of the conditions of women in post-apartheid South Africa. It has a quarterly publication, *Gender Matters*, which discusses in detail the interests and works of the commission. According to the editor, *Gender Matters* "is an information exchange vehicle, which we trust academics, gender activists, government and all relevant stakeholders will utilise to evaluate, monitor and set standards for the protection and promotion of gender equality."[370] The maiden issue of *Gender Matters* was published in December 2000 and undertook

---

365 Background to the CGE, http://www.cge.org.za/about/backgrnd.htm, page 1 of 3.
366 Ibid., 1.
367 CGE Vision and Mission Statement, http://www.cge.org.za/about/vision.htm, 1, Commission on Gender Equality in *Gender Matters*, v.1, (October–December 2000), 4.
368 CGE Vision and Mission Statement, http://www.cge.org.za/about/vision.htm, 1 of 2.
369 CGE Vision and Mission Statement, http://www.cge.org.za/about/vision.htm, 1. Commission on Gender Equality in *Gender Matters*, 4.
370 Editor's Note in *Gender Matters*, v.1, (October–December 2000), 2.

a thorough analysis of the activities, successes, and challenges of the Commission on Gender Equity at the dawn of the new millennium.

The CGE works with the general public, Non-governmental Organizations (NGOs), the major political parties (i.e., the ANC, the GNU, and the Democratic Party), and the South African parliament to achieve its goals.[371] It also works with local and international groups to support rural women and recognize their contributions to post-apartheid South Africa. On World Rural Women's Day (October 15), it joined the international community in honoring the achievements of South Africa's rural women. These poor rural women are often single parents and Black women who occupy the bottom of the socioeconomic ladder in South Africa. It will take a complete overhaul of the system to turn things around for them. Commenting on the importance of this annual event, *Gender Matters* states that this is

> the only day in the calendar of the world that gives recognition to the most marginalised of all, rural women. They are the unsung heroes of yesterday and today. No award winning novels, history books or even praise songs even consider their existence let alone their contribution . . . we owe the development of our communities to these forgotten heroines. Yet with all their outstanding contribution they continue to suffer the most.[372]

Other major issues addressed by CGE include power sharing between men and women in the local communities, land tenure, domestic violence, and gender equity in political parties. It also addresses such gender issues as government recognition of Islamic marriages and other customary marriages, virginity testing, HIV/AIDS, teenage pregnancy,

---

371 Joyce Piliso-Seroke in *Gender Matters*, 3; Commission on Gender Equality in *Gender Matters*, 4.
372 Commission on Gender Equality, "Rural Women Join the Global Campaign in the Fight Against Poverty" in *Gender Matters*, 11.

and portrayal of women in the media, to mention but a few.[373] The Commission is charged with the responsibility to work with relevant parties to eradicate institutionalized sexism in the school system, the legal system, the marketplace, the religious sphere, the economic sector, and the political system.[374]

The CGE has continued to monitor both national and local elections with a special interest in gender representation. According to *Country Status Report - Inequality in Sharing Power & Decision*, during the apartheid period, women were poorly represented in South African politics, but today gender representation has improved. For example, in 1985, "only 2.8% of parliamentarians were women."[375] Concurring with the above report, *Gender Matters* states that "before South Africa's first democratic elections in 1994, women constituted a mere 2.7% of MPs. Currently, women make up 29.75% of the National Assembly compared to 27.7% in 1994."[376] While this represents a significant improvement in the levels of women's participation in government prior to the end of apartheid, the gap remains significantly wide, since women currently make up 55 percent of 18,476,519 registered voters in South Africa. We are still a long way from the point when women's voting power will translate to a major power shift in favor of their group in the South African government (see chapter 2).[377]

Although the commission has recorded some achievements in terms of its efforts on behalf of women, it is still faced with the challenge of getting society to recognize the gravity of problems associated with institutionalized sexism and gender inequality. So far greater attention has been devoted to the issues of race and racism in post-apartheid South Africa. Commenting on this state of affairs, the chief executive

---

373 Commission on Gender Equality, "Notable Achievements in 2000" in *Gender Matters*, 4; Futhi Zikalala, "Provincial Spotlight: Kwa-Zulu Natal" in *Gender Matters*, 10.
374 Joyce Piliso-Seroke, "Reflections on the Conference: Combating Racism, A Nation in Dialogue" in *Gender Matters*, 5.
375 *Country Status Report - Inequality in Sharing Power & Decision*, http://www.sn.apc.org/beijing/stpower.htm, page 2 of 7.
376 Fatima Seedat, "Parliamentary Update" in *Gender Matters*, 12.
377 Election News: Independent Election Commission in *Gender Matters*, 14.

officer of the commission, in a recent interview with Face to Face, stated he was "actually disappointed" by what he described as a huge regression in gender advancement. There is little solace in the fact that the commission's mandate is limited to monitoring and making recommendations to the parliament as opposed to taking a "pro-active stance to eliminate gender discrimination."[378] Other problems related to inadequate staffing of the commission and inadequate training of employees in gender-friendly service delivery. Perhaps one of the most serious challenges faced by the commission is related to the negative perception of its mission by men. This is most clearly shown by allegations that the commission has colluded with the government in promoting anti-male policies.[379]

The history of South Africa displays a remarkable degree of continuity and discontinuity pertaining to the experience of women, especially Black women. In precolonial society, Black women were not entitled to equal rights and privileges as men. For the most part, they had a limited opportunity to participate in politics; women did not serve on the chief's council. This was because women were not expected to play leadership roles in their communities. They were expected to "leave words" to the men. Women in precolonial South Africa looked up to their male relatives for farm land since the land tenure system did not allow them to own land. Similarly, they were not allowed to own cattle, which was a major economic commodity or source of wealth.

During the apartheid period, Black women were treated as legal minors. As a result, they continued to depend on their male relatives for land and housing. Women could not own lands and did not qualify to be taxpayers, while their sons, upon turning eighteen, qualified and were automatically required to pay taxes, which qualified them as adults and leaders in their respective families and communities. Once the sons of Black women turned eighteen, they could obtain government housing, own land, and enter into contracts with other people. In

---

378 Zith Mahaye, "Face to Face" in *Gender Matters*, 9.
379 Ibid.

addition, they could be appointed to various government positions, especially in the reserves.

In the face of their collective plight, Black women have historically used both their personal and group experiences to encourage each other and to resist oppression. In precolonial South Africa, Mmanthatisi of the Sotho people, upon her husband's death, convinced the elders to accept her as a regent, and she proved to be a dynamic leader. She demonstrated that women could be good leaders if given the opportunity. In this sense, she was a role model to future generations of Black women in South Africa, and there is no doubt that she was a source of inspiration to contemporary South African women. During the apartheid period, Black women leaders like Lilian Ngoyi, Emma Mashinini, Winnie Mandela, Albertina Sisulu, and Ruth Mampati, to mention but a few, used their personal stories to encourage other women to carry on with the struggle against racial oppression.

Since the end of apartheid in 1994, the new multiracial government has taken remarkable steps to reverse the situation of women by adopting one of the most democratic constitutions in the modern world. South Africa is positioned to be a model in the areas of racial and gender equity and national reconciliation to the extent that the relevant constitutional provisions are implemented faithfully. The government has created the Commission on Gender Equality, the first of its kind in modern Africa. The commission focuses on gender issues such as rape, domestic violence, discriminatory customs, maternity leave, virginity testing, and the conditions of women in rural communities. Women can file complaints at the commission when they are victimized in these and similar areas. This is a historic opportunity for Black women in South Africa to regain their dignity.

Despite recent changes noted in this chapter, South Africa has yet to become a safe haven for women. The country has taken positive constitutional steps that hold out the promise of a beautiful future for women, but the negative tendencies associated with racism and sexism are resilient. Many South African men and women are still in denial about gender issues. Even some Blacks find it difficult to acknowledge that there are gender problems that are as important as racial discrimination. Also, some South African men, including Black men, do not believe that women should be entitled to equal rights as men. These problems are compounded by the fact that the Commission on Gender Equality has limited powers; while it can be an advocate for women, it does not have an autonomous status, and its mandate is limited to monitoring situations and making recommendations to parliament. In practical terms, the commission has not recorded much progress in terms of resolving problems facing women. Against this backdrop, it should be noted that South Africa became a democratic state barely seven years ago. Not only does it need more time, but also a major shift away from traditional attitudes toward women, by both the leaders and the general public, in order to effectively implement new policies that are expected to bring about some of the changes that Black women and other anti-apartheid groups struggled for. As it is always said, no country is built in one day. If the present state of affairs calls for patience, it also calls for relentless vigilance on the part of South African women and their allies, at home and abroad. Even in older democracies, there is always a great need for governments to be pressured by interest groups in order for the latter to have their needs met. In this respect, there is an abundance of political lessons from other African countries where post-colonial governments unabashedly reneged on promises made to their people in the course of the anti-colonial struggle pertaining to democracy, human rights, and economic justice.

BIBLIOGRAPHY

Aardt, M. Van, and Sadie Y. "Women's Issues in South Africa: 1990–1994." *Africa Insight* vol. 25, no. 2 (1995): 80–90.

Adam, Heribert, and Kogila Moodley. "Comparing South Africa: Nonracialism versus Ethnonationalist Revival." *Third World Quarterly* vol. 14, no. 2 (1993): 339–350.

Baines, Gary. "The Contradictions of Community Politics: The African Petty Bourgeoisie and the New Brighton Advisory Board, c. 1937–1952." *Journal of African History* vol. 35 (1994): 79–97.

Barrett, Jane, et al. *Southern African Women on the Move.* London: Catholic Institute for International Relations, 1985.

Benson, Mary. *The Struggle in South Africa Has United All Races.* New York: United Nations Centre Against Apartheid: Notes and Documents, August 1984.

Berger, Iris. *Threads of Solidarity: Women in South African Industry 1900–1980.* Bloomington: Indiana University Press, 1992.

———. *Sources of Class Consciousness: The Experience of Women Workers in South Africa, 1973–1980.* African Studies Center Working Papers, no. 55. Boston University, October 21–24, 1981.

Bernstein, Hilda. *For Their Triumphs and For Their Tears: Conditions and Resistance of Women in Apartheid South Africa.* International Defence & Aid Fund, August 1975.

Bickford-Smith, Vivian. "Black Ethnicities, Communities and Political Expression in Late Victorian Cape Colony." *Journal of African History* vol. 36 (1995): 443–465.

———. "Commerce, Class and Ethnicity: Cape Town at the Advent of the Mineral Revolution (c. 1875)." *Social Dynamics* vol. 13, no. 32 (1987): 32–45.

Bischoff, Paul-Henri. "1994 and Beyond: Parameters of Change in Southern Africa." *Africa Insight* vol. 25, no. 2 (1995): 108–114.

Bozzoli, Belinda. "Marxism, Feminism and South African Studies." *Journal of Southern Africa Studies* vol. 9, no. 2 (April 1983): 139–171.

———. *Women of Phokeng: Consciousness, Life Strategy, and Migration in South Africa, 1900–1983.* (Portsmouth, NH: Heinemann, A Division of Reed Elsevier, Inc., 1991).

Bradford, Helen. "Women, Gender and Colonialism: Rethinking the History of the British Cape Colony and its Frontier Zone, c. 1806–70." *Journal of African History* vol. 37 (1996): 371–418.

Bullwinkle, Davis A. *Women of Eastern and Southern Africa: A Bibliography, 1976– 1985, African Special Bibliographic Series, Number II.* New York: Greenwood Press, 1989.

Chamberlain, M. E. *The Scramble for Africa.* London: Longman Group Limited, 1974.

Christenson, Ronald. "The Civil Religion of Apartheid: Afrikanerdom's Covenant." *Midwest Quarterly* vol. 20, no. 2 (Winter 1979): 137–146.

Cock, Jacklyn. *Maids and Madams: A Study in the Politics of Exploitation.* Johannesburg: Raven Press, 1980.

Cole, Josette. *Crossroads: The Politics of Reform and Repression, 1976–1986.* Johannesburg: Ravan Press, 1987.

Commission on Gender Equality. http://www.cge.org.za/about/backgrnd.htm.

Constitution of the Republic of South Africa http://polity.org.za/govdocs/constitution/saconst.html.

Coombes, Annie E. "Gender, 'Race,' Ethnicity in Art Practice in Post-Apartheid South Africa: Annie E. Coombes and Penny Siopis in Conversation." *Feminist Review*, no. 55 (Spring 1997): 110–129.

Coquery-Vidrovitch, Catherine. *African Women: A Modern History.* Boulder: Westview Press, 1997.

Country Status Report - Inequality in Shaping Power & Decision. http://www.sn.apc.org/beijing/stpower.htm.

Curtin, Philip D. "The Environment Beyond Europe and the European Theory of Empire." *Journal of World History* vol. 1, no. 2 (1990): 131–150.

———, et al. *African History From Earliest Times to Independence.* Second Edition. New York: Longman Publishing, 1995.

Davis, Stephen M. *Apartheid's Rebels: Inside South Africa's Hidden War.* New Haven: Yale University Press, 1987.

Daymond, Margaret J. "Class in the Discources of Sindiwe Magona's Autobiography and Fiction." *Journal of Southern African Studies* vol. 21, no. 4 (December 1985): 561–572.

Driver, Dorothy. "Imagined Selves, (Un)imagined Marginalities." *Journal of Southern African Studies* vol. 17, no. 2 (June 1991): 337–354.

Ellis, Stephen, and Tsepo Sechaba. *Comrades Against Apartheid: The ANC & the South African Communist Party in Exile.* London: James Currey Ltd., 1992.

Feit, Edward. *African Opposition in South Africa: The Failure of Passive Resistance.* Stanford, CA: Hoover Institution Publication, 1967.

Frates, Lioys L. "Women in the South African National Liberation Movement, 1948– 1960: An Historiographical Review." *Ufahamu: Journal of the South African Activist Association* vol. 21, no. 1–2 (1993): 27–40.

Frederikse, Julie. *The Unbreakable Thread: Non-Racialism in South Africa.* Bloomington, IN: Indiana University Press, 1990.

Gailey, Harry A. *History of Africa from 1800 to Present.* New York: Holt, Rinehart and Winston, Inc., 1972.

Gaitskell, Deborah. "Christian Compounds for Girls: Church Hostels for African Women in Johannesburg, 1907–1970." *Journal of Southern African Studies* vol. 6, no. 1 (1979): 44–69.

Gender Matters. Quarterly by the Commission on Gender Equality vol. 1 (October– December, 2000).

Gerhart, Gail M. *Black Power in South Africa: The Evolution of An Ideology.* Berkeley: University of California Press, 1978.

Goodman, June. *Cry Amandla: South African Women and the Question of Power.* New York: Africana Publishing Company, 1984.

Goodwin, June. "Christianity and Conflicts in South Africa." *Christianity and Crises* vol. 44, no. 9 (May 28, 1984): 200.

Gordon, Elizabeth. "An Analysis of the Impact of Labour Migration on the Lives of Women in Lesotho." *Journal of Development Studies* vol. 17 (October 1980–July 1981): 59–76.

Hay, Margaret, and Sharon Stichter (ed). *African Women South of the Sahara*. New York: Longman Inc., 1984.

Helly, Dorothy O. "'Informed' Opinion on Tropical Africa in Great Britain 1860–1890." *African Affairs* vol. 68, no. 272 (1969): 195–217.

Hetherington, Penelope. "Women in South Africa: The Historiography in English." *The International Journal of African Historical Studies* vol. 26, no. 2 (1993): 241–270.

Hirschmann, David. "Urban Women, Civil Society, and Social Transition in the Eastern Cape, South Africa." *African Rural and Urban Studies* vol. 1, no. 2 (1994): 31–48.

Holland, Heidi. *The Struggle: A History of African National Congress*. New York: George Braziller, Inc., 1989.

Hyslop, Jonathan. "White Working-Class Women and the Invention of Apartheid: 'Purified' Afrikaner Nationalist Agitation for Legislation Against 'Mixed' Marriages, 1934–9." *Journal of African History* vol. 36 (1995): 57–81.

Isichei, Elizabeth. *From Antiquity to the Present: A History of Christianity in Africa*. Grand Rapids, Michigan: William B. Eerdmans Publishing Company, 1995.

Johnson, David. "Aspects of a Liberal Education: Late Nineteenth-Century Attitudes to Race, from Cambridge to the Cape Colony." *History Workshop Journal* (1993): 162–182.

July, Robert W. *A History of the African People.* Fifth Edition. Prospect Heights, Illinois: Waveland Press, Inc., 1998.

Kinsman, Margaret. "Beasts of Burden: The Subordination of Southern Tswana Women, ca 1800–1840." *A Journal of Southern African Studies* vol. 10, no. 1 (October, 1983): 39–54.

Klandermans, Bert, Marlene Roefs, and Johan Olivier. "Politics Protest and Political Transition in South Africa." *Africa Studies* vol. 56, no. 1 (1997): 129–155.

Konczacka, Janina M. "The Role of Natal in the Development of the Policy of Racial Segregation in South Africa in the Nineteenth and Early Twentieth Century." *Africana Bulletin* vol. 33, (1986): 51–63.

Krebs, Paula M. "The Last of the Gentlemen's Wars: Women in the Boer War Concentration Camp." *History Workshop* issue 33 (1992): 38–56.

Kuper, Leo. *Passive Resistance in South Africa.* New Haven, CT: Yale University Press, 1957.

Kuzwayo, Ellen. *Call Me Woman.* San Francisco: Spinsters Ink, 1985.

Lanegran, Kimberly. "South Africa's Civic Association Movement: ANC's Ally or Society's 'Watchdog'? Shifting Social Movement-Political Party Relations." *African Studies Review* vol. 38, no. 2 (September 1995): 101–126.

Lapchick, Richard E., and Stephanie Urdang. *Oppression and Resistance: The Struggle of Women in Southern Africa.* West Port, CT: Greenwood Press, 1982.

Lazar, Carol. *A Single Photograph, a Thousand Words.* Boston: Little, Brown and Company Inc., 1993.

Lemon, Anthony. *Apartheid in Transition.* Boulder, CO: Westview Press, 1987.

Makhoere, Caesarina Kona. *No Child's Play: In Prison Under Apartheid.* London: The Women's Press, Ltd., 1988.

Mandela, Nelson. *Long Walk to Freedom: The Autobiography of Nelson Mandela.* Boston: Little, Brown and Company, 1994.

Mandela, Winnie. *Part of My Soul Went with Him.* New York: W. W. Norton & Company, 1985.

Marks, Shula, (ed.). *Not Either An Experimental Doll: The Separate Worlds of Three South African Women.* Bloomington: Indiana University Press, 1987.

———. "Khoisan Resistance to the Dutch in the Seventeenth Century and Eighteenth Centuries." *Journal of African History* vol. 13, no. 1 (1972): 55–80.

———, and Stanley Trapido (ed.). *The Politics of Race, Class and Nationalism in Twentieth Century South Africa.* England: Longman Group UK Limited, 1987.

Martin, Phyllis, M., and Patrick O'Meara. *Africa.* Third Edition. Bloomington, IN: University Press, 1995.

Marx, Anthony W. *Lessons of Struggle: South African International Opposition, 1960– 1990.* New York: Oxford University Press, 1992.

Marquard, Leo. *The Peoples and Policies of South Africa.* Third Edition. London: Oxford University Press, 1962.

Mashinini, Emma. *Strikes Have Followed Me All My Life: A South African Autobiography.* New York: Routledge, 1991.

McCuen, Gary E. *The Apartheid Reader: Ideals in Conflict Series.* Hudson, WI: Gary McCuen Publications Inc., 1986.

Meer, Fatima. *Women in the Apartheid Society.* New York: United Nations Centre Against Apartheid: Notes and Documents, April 1985.

Mermelstein, David. *The Anti-Apartheid Reader: The Struggle Against White Racist Rule in South Africa.* New York: Grove Press, 1987.

Morris, Alan. "Fighting Against the Tide: The White Right and Desegregation in Johannesburg's Inner City." *African Studies* vol. 57, no. 1 (1998): 55–78.

Nelson, Nici (ed.). *African Women in the Development Process.* Great Britain: Frank Cass and Company Ltd., 1981.

Ngubane, Jordan K. *An African Explains Apartheid.* New York: Frederick A. Praeger Publisher, 1963.

Nnaemeka, Obioma, (ed). *Sisterhood: Feminism & Power From Africa to the Diaspora.* New Jersey: Africa World Press, Inc., 1998.

O'Brien, Colleen. "The Search for Mother Africa: Poetry Revises Women's Struggle for Freedom." *Africa Studies Review* vol. 37, no. 2 (1994): 147–155.

Ogden, Susan P. *Africa South of the Sahara*. Fifteenth Edition. London: Europa Publications, Ltd., 1989.

Omer-Cooper, J. D. *History of Southern Africa*. Portsmouth, NH: Heinemann Educational Books, Inc., 1987.

"Oppression of Black Women in Apartheid South Africa." *The Ethiopian Herald*, 30 September, 1981.

Papandreou, Margarita. "Decade for Women; Nairobi, July 16, 1985." *Atlantis* vol. 12, no. 2 (Spring/Printemps 1987): 103–107.

Perold, Helene. *Working Women: A Portrait of South Africa's Black Women Workers*. Johannesburg: Ravan Press (Pty) Ltd., 1985.

Platzky, Laurine, and Cheryl Walker. *The Surplus People: Forced Removals in South Africa*. Johannesburg: Raven Press, 1985.

Porter, Andrew. "Cambridge, Keswick, and Late-Nineteenth-Century Attitudes to Africa." *The Journal of Imperial and Commonwealth History* vol. 5, no. 1 (1976): 5–34.

Praha, Jaroslav Cesar. "The Role of Racial Elements in Establishing the Ideology of British Imperialism." *Archiv Orientalni* vol. 44 (1976): 97–125.

Redding, Sean. "Legal Minors and Social Children: Rural African Women and Taxation in the Transkei, South Africa." *African Studies Review* vol. 36, no. 3 (December 1993): 49–74.

Redehr, Ernie. *Perceptions of Apartheid: The Churches and Political Change in South Africa.* Scottdale, PA: Herald Press, 1979.

Rogers, Mirabel. *The Black Sash: The Story of the South African Women's Defence of the Constitution League.* Johannesburg: Rotonews (Pty.) Ltd., 1956

Rogerson, M. "Periodic Markets and Rural Development in South Africa." *Africa Insight* vol. 27, no. 2 (1987): 98–111.

―――. "Local Government and the SMME in South African Economy." *Africa Insight* vol. 27, no. 1 (1997): 63–72.

Rottenberg, Paula S. *Racism and Sexism: An Integrated Study.* New York: St. Martin Press, 1988.

Roux, Edward. *Time Longer Than Rope: A History of the Black Man's Struggle for Freedom in South Africa.* Madison: The University of Wisconsin Press (1964).

Russell, Diana E. H. *Lives of Courage: Women For A New South Africa.* New York: Basic Books, 1989.

Sapire, Hilary. "Apartheid's 'Testing Ground': Urban 'Native Policy' and African Politics in Brakpan, South Africa, 1943–1948." *Journal of African History* vol. 35 (1994): 99–123.

Saunders, Christopher. "American and South African Black History: Comparisons and Connections." *African Studies* vol. 57, no. 1 (1998): 113–117.

Saunders, C. C. "The Recognition of African Law: The Cape in the Nineteenth Century." *African Perspectives* vol. 2 (1979): 89–95.

Schirmer, Stefan. "What Would We Be Without Our Land and Cattle?": Migrations, Land, Labour Tenants in Mpumalanga, 1940–1950." *African Studies* vol. 55, no. 1 (1996): 111–138.

Schmidt, Elizabeth. *Decoding Corporate Camouflage: US Business Support for Apartheid.* Washington, DC: Institute for Policy Studies, 1980.

Scully, Pamela. "Rape, Race, and Colonial Culture: The Sexual Politics of Identity in the Nineteenth-Century Cape Colony, South Africa." *American Historical Review* vol. 100, no. 2 (1995): 335–359.

Shelby, John. *A Short History of South Africa.* London: George Allen & Unwin Ltd., 1973.

Smith, David M. (ed). *Separation in South Africa: People and Policies.* Occasional Papers, No. 6, Department of Geography, Queen Mary College, University of London (March 1976).

Stuart, Doug. "For England and For Christ: The Gospel of Liberation and Subordination in Early Nineteenth Century Southern Africa." *Journal of Historical Sociology* vol. 6, no. 4 (1993): 377–395.

Sweetman, David. *Women Leaders in African History.* Portsmouth, NH: Heinemann Educational Book Inc., 1984.

Theal, George M. *The History of South Africa.* London: G. P. Putman's & Sons, 1894.

Thompson, Leonard M. *A History of South Africa.* Revised Edition. New Haven: Yale University Press, 1995.

———. *The Republic of South Africa.* Boston: Little, Brown and Company, 1966.

———, and Jeffrey Butler (ed). *Change in Contemporary South Africa.* Berkeley: University of California Press, 1975.

To Honor Women's Day: Profiles of Leading Women in the South African and Namibian Struggles. Cambridge, MA: International Defence and Aid Fund for Southern Africa in Co-operation with United Nations Centre Against Apartheid (1981).

Tripathy, Joshodhara. "Plight of Black Women in South Africa: Feminism Reinforced Sans Humanism." *Africa Quarterly* vol. xxiv, nos. 3–4 (1985): 52–71.

United Nations Centre Against Apartheid: Notes and Documents. April 1985.

Van Vuuren, Nancy. *Women Against Apartheid: The Fight for Freedom in South Africa, 1920–1975.* Palo Alto, CA: Robert D. Reed and Adams A. Eterovich, 1979.

Waldman, Linda. "Monkey in a Spiderweb: The Dynamics of Farmer Control and Paternalism." *Africa Studies* vol. 55, no. 1 (1996): 63–86.

Walker, Cherryl. *Women and Resistance in South Africa.* London: Onyx Press, 1982.

Walshe, Peter. *The Rise of African Nationalism in South Africa: The African National Congress 1912–1952.* Berkeley and Los Angeles: University of California Press, 1971.

Wells, Julia C. "Why Women Rebel: A Comparative Study of South African Women's Resistance in Bloemfontein (1913) and

Johannesburg (1958)." *Journal of Southern African Studies* vol. 10, no. 1 (October 1983).

Wheyl, Nathaniel. *Traitor's End: The Rise and Fall of the Communist Movement in Southern Africa.* New York: Allington House, 1970.

Willen, Richard S. "Normative Structure of South African Inequality." *Free Inquiry in Creative Sociology* vol. 10, no. 1 (May 1982), pp 80–84.

Wiss, Rosemary. "Lipreading: Remembering Saartjie Baartman." *The Australian Journal of Anthropology* vol. 5, no. 1–2 (1994): 11–40.

Young, Robert J. C. "Black Athena: The Politics of Scholarship." *Science as Culture* vol. 4, no. 2 (1993): 274–281.

INDEX

A

Achilles heel of South Africa, 109
actions, government's, 57, 62
adulthood, 18, 47, 49
adults, vii, 14, 19, 21, 23, 26, 47, 73, 115, 119
Africa, 3, 32, 35, 54–55, 124, 126, 129–32
Africa Insight vol, 123–24, 132
African children, 52, 64
African families, 79, 111
African groups, 38, 53
African National Congress. See ANC
African National Congress Women's League, 8, 80–82
African Nationalism in South Africa, 39, 42, 134
African Opposition in South Africa, 126
African People, 22, 40, 82, 128
Africans, 34, 38–41, 47–53, 65, 73, 76, 79, 107–8, 110–11, 123, 130
African Studies, 45, 65
African Studies Review, 45, 47
African Studies Review vol, 128, 131
African Studies vol, 130, 132–33
African Women, 3, 8–9, 51, 58, 61, 101, 125, 130
  contemporary South, 120
  marrying South, 34
African women and Asian women, 36
African Women's Association (AWA), 80
African Women South, 127
African Women's Resistance, 134
African women teachers, 70

Afrikaans, 42, 83–84, 95
Afrikaans language, 53, 63–64
Afrikaner Nationalism, 42–44
Afrikaners, 1, 4–5, 32, 35, 38–43, 111
Afrikaner women, 5
  most, 5
age, 14, 21, 29, 49, 58, 81, 95, 114–15
agreement, 26, 94
Albertina, 83, 86–90
Albertina Sisulu, 5, 59, 83, 85, 120
Allied Workers Union of South Africa, ix
Alverson, Hoyt, 28
ANC (African National Congress), 5, 7, 9, 13, 40, 58, 63, 77, 80–82, 85, 88, 98–99, 103, 117, 126, 134
ANC members, 98
ANCWL (ANC Women's League), 5, 8–9, 80–82, 86
ANCWL African National Congress Women's League AZAPO Azanian, ix
ANC Women's League. See ANCWL
anti-apartheid activist, full-time, 96
anti-apartheid activists, 59, 87
  committed White, 93
anti-apartheid activities, 76
anti-apartheid organizations, 75–76, 81, 88
  formed, 80
  inclusive, 80
  mainstream, 5
  most inclusive women's, 101
Anti-Apartheid Reader, 63–64, 130
Anti-apartheid sentiments, 108

apartheid, v, vii, 1–7, 9–14, 17–19, 21, 23, 25, 27, 33, 39–41, 43–45, 51–55, 57, 63–67, 69, 71–83, 85–97, 99–107, 109–13, 117–21, 123–24, 126–27, 129–30, 132–34
  architects of, 1, 5
  dismantle, 5, 76, 82, 95, 101
  dismantling, 14
  supported, 5, 11, 63
  term, 72
apartheid agents, 64
apartheid authorities, 85
apartheid era, 11–12, 52, 73, 102
apartheid government, 10, 56, 59–60, 72, 94
apartheid ideology, 54, 61
apartheid laws, v, 3, 32–33, 53, 71, 80, 93, 102, 106
  dismantle, 64
  repeal, 13
apartheid period, 10, 85, 118–20
apartheid police, 12, 64, 97
apartheid police agents, 92
apartheid policies, 4–5, 9, 13–14, 75, 82–83
  resist, 83
Apartheid Reader, 55, 62–63, 74, 77, 80
The Apartheid Reader, Gary E., 130
apartheid regime, 3–4, 6–7, 11–12, 14, 57, 59–60, 76, 79, 87, 92, 99, 106, 115
apartheid rule, vii, 56, 76, 92, 97, 105
apartheid security agents, 83, 88, 96
apartheid security o"cers, 11
Apartheid Society, 130
Apartheid South Africa, 4, 6, 11, 55–57, 71, 82, 86, 91, 106, 125
Apartheid's Rebels, Stephen M., 125
apartheid state, 106

apartheid system, viii, 2–4, 49, 61–62, 64, 66–67, 69, 77, 82, 86, 88, 96, 107, 111, 113
Apartheid to Multiracial Democracy, vi, 106
area
  residential, 52, 59–60
  urban, 50–52, 73, 77
arrangements, 2, 50, 61, 66, 110
arrests, 9, 11–12, 14, 93
arrival, vii, 17–18, 30, 35, 98
attention, 3, 35–36, 93, 118
attitudes, 5, 131
Australia, 108
authorities, 17, 26, 37, 59, 64, 84–85, 88–89, 97
AWA (African Women's Association), 80

B

baby, 6, 49, 69, 83, 87
bands, 16, 26–27
Bantu, 16–17, 27
Bantu Authorities Act, 13, 60–61
Bantu Education Act, 60–64
Bantu Education Act for Black women, 64
Bantu teachers, 70
basis, 5, 31, 45, 64, 77
Beasts of Burden, 15, 28–30, 128
beaten, 46, 52, 73, 96
bene°ts, 29, 44, 114–15
Benson, Mary, 2, 11–12, 89
Bernstein, Hilda, 104
Bibliography, vi, 123–24
Biko, 96, 99
Biko, Steve, 96–97, 100
Black activists, young, 62
Black adults, 46
Black and White males, vii
Black and White schools, 61

Black Athena, 135
Black athletes, 62
Black children, 7, 46, 62–64, 67–68, 89
  denied, 62
  innocent, 88
Black communities, 45, 56, 67, 72, 88
Black community of Sophiatown, 79
Black Consciousness, 81, 96, 99
Black Consciousness Movement, 80–81, 96, 98–99
Black doctor, 79
Black dropout children, unfortunate, 69
Black educators, 63
Black employees, 12, 47, 90
Black Ethnicities, 124
Black families, 9–10, 14, 51–52, 65–67, 79
  most, 65
Black female activists, 57, 83
Black female factory workers, 70
Black females, 49, 70
Black girls, 66
Black homelands, 7, 109
Black households, 47
Black industrial workers, 11
Black labor, 14
  cheap, 47
Black laborers, 45, 65
Black laborers and White employers, 45
Black labor unionist, 51
Black male children, 66
Black male leaders, 100
Black mothers, 52, 62, 84, 115
Black nannies, 68
Black nationalism, 99
Black Nationalist Center, 96
Black neighborhoods, 14
Black nurses, 71, 86
Black opponents, 12
Black parents, 46, 62, 64, 66, 106
  exhorted, 83

Black Parents Association, 84
Black Parents' Association, 83
black peril, 95
Black population, 47, 72
Black Power, Gail M., 126
Black residential area, 8
Black residential quarters, 50
Blacks, vii, 3–6, 11–12, 14, 31, 33, 40, 42–43, 45–46, 48–50, 52, 54, 59, 61–62, 66–67, 72, 79–80, 91–92, 97–99, 107, 110–11, 113, 120–21, 131–32
  fellow, 90
  restricted, 48
Black Sash, 76, 80, 89, 132
Black schoolchildren, 7, 62, 64, 76, 106–7
  provoked, 84
Black schools, 63
Black South Africans, 5, 7, 17, 44, 50, 77, 79
Black teachers, 63, 70–71
Black trade unions, 12
Black unionists, 12
Black university students, 108
Black urban population, stable, 51
Black victims, 10
Black woman, 10, 94
  banished, 57
Black Women, v–viii, 3, 5–9, 11–15, 17–19, 21, 23, 25, 27–35, 37–39, 41–49, 51–53, 55–57, 59–61, 63–73, 75–77, 79–83, 85–87, 89, 91, 101–7, 109–13, 115, 117, 119–21
  forced, 46, 68
  married, 9, 14
  sons of, 47, 119
Black Women and Apartheid Laws, v, 53
Black women and White domination, 33
Black Women and White Domination, v, 44

Black women in South Africa, 72, 120
Black women leaders, 100, 120
Black women's contributions, 100–101
Black women's e'orts, 7
Black women's experiences, vii, 3
Black Women's Federation, 83
Black women's liberation struggle, 3
Black Women's Response, v, 74
Black women's struggles, vii, 112, 115
Black women su'er, 3
Black Women Workers, 28, 49, 91
Black workers, 7, 11–12, 90, 92, 94
  industrial, 12
Black workers in South Africa, 91
Black workers in South African industry, 10
Bloemfontein, 7–8, 134
Bloomington, 123, 126, 129
Boston, 7, 62, 64, 75, 79, 129, 134
Botha, 42, 110
boys, 14, 18–19, 21–23, 30, 34
  responsible Black, 66
bread, 32
Britain, 37, 39, 42, 127, 130
British, 31, 38–41
Broederbond, 41, 43–44
bull, 21–22
burying, 49
butterfat, 21–22

C

ca, 15, 126, 128, 134
Caesarina Kona Makhoere, 10–11, 44
Caeserina Makhoere, 67, 69
Cambridge, 75, 128, 131, 134
campaign, women's anti-pass, 9
Cape, 35, 37, 40, 43, 52, 59, 72, 132
Cape Colony, 15, 37, 39, 128
Cape of Good Hope, vii, 34–35
Cape of South Africa, 16

Cape Town, 110–11, 124
care, 16, 27, 30, 36, 47, 64, 68–69, 72, 75, 87
cases, 25–27, 46–47, 52, 58, 65, 69
cattle, 15–17, 24–25, 27, 30, 34, 36–37, 44, 65–66, 119, 133
CCAWUSA (Commercial, Catering, and Allied Workers' Union of South Africa), 12, 80–81, 91
centrality, 2–3, 106
century, 4, 7, 34, 37, 39, 82
ceremonies, 20–21
  religious, 20
CGE (Commission on Gender Equality), 14, 104, 116–18, 120–21, 125
CGE Vision and Mission Statement, 116
Change in Contemporary South Africa, 134
Change in South Africa, 132
Cherryl Walker, 51, 60–61, 101
chiefdoms, 17, 21, 26–27
Chief Luspance, 34
chiefs, 17, 21, 23–27, 29–30, 60–61, 118
Child, 10–11, 44, 53, 68–69, 129
children, 10, 18, 27, 30, 33–34, 41, 44, 46–47, 64, 66–71, 73, 75, 77, 80, 83–86, 89–90, 101, 106, 115
  eir, 64
Christianity, 54, 127
Christianity and Con‚ict in South Africa, 54
Christianity and Con‚icts in South Africa, 127
church, 76, 90–91
Church Hostels for African Women in Johannesburg, 126
churchwomen, 87
cities, 44, 51–52, 67, 77, 92, 107, 110–11
citizens, 4, 13, 57, 113, 115
  full, 115

citizenship, 23, 115
Civil Religion of Apartheid, 124
clans, 17, 26
class, vii, 6, 31, 44–45, 49, 77, 81, 99, 105, 113, 116, 124–25, 129
clergy, 76
click languages, 16–17
Cock, 7, 68–69, 125
Cock, Jacklyn, 33, 68
Colored, 6, 56, 59, 70, 76, 107, 110
Commercial, Catering, and Allied Workers' Union of South Africa (CCAWUSA), 12, 80–81, 91
commission, 116, 118–21
Commission on Gender Equality. *See* CGE
Commission on Gender Equality in Gender Matters, 116–17
communism, 57
communists, 12, 59, 87, 98
communities, 17–18, 20–24, 27, 30, 51, 66, 72, 82, 96–97, 102, 117, 119, 124
Company, 7, 62, 64, 79, 129, 134
Comparative Study of South African Women, 7
conditions, vii, 30, 33, 67–68, 73, 90, 104–5, 107, 123
  working, 11–12, 65, 90
Conditions and Resistance of Women in Apartheid South Africa, 104, 123
conditions of women, 116, 120
conference, 101, 118
Conflict Series, 55, 62–63, 74, 130
Congress of South African Trade Unions (COSATU), 80, 94
constitution, vi, 14, 112–16, 125
  new, 5, 105, 111–13
contact, iv, 34–35
Contemporary South Africa, 33, 134
context, 13, 61, 65, 76–77, 81

contrast, sharp, 52, 60–61
contributions, vii, 3, 9, 20, 41, 71, 73, 76, 105, 117
  women's, 3, 83
control, 18, 39, 46–47, 52, 61, 65–67, 84, 134
COSATU (Congress of South African Trade Unions), 80, 94
COSATU Congress of South African Trade Unions, ix
counselors, 23–25, 61
country, viii, 1, 7, 15, 35, 41, 62, 72, 84, 89, 97, 100–101, 105, 109, 113, 120–21
Country Status Report, 118, 125
Courage, 7, 66, 76, 83, 85–87, 89, 91, 93, 96, 103, 132
court, 2, 25, 30, 45–46, 73, 97
court cases, 28
cows, 22, 29–30, 36
creation, 38, 50, 58, 110
crisis, 54, 99, 109
Cry Amandla, 1, 5, 11–13, 28, 56–57, 62, 68, 81, 95–96, 98–99, 126
CT, 128–29

D

daughters, xi, 11, 24, 29, 64
David, 127–28, 130, 133
death, 9, 49, 97, 100
democracies, 116, 121
demonstrations, women's, 58
detainees, 93, 96
detentions, 12, 14, 93, 96, 106, 115
deteriorate, 107–8
disability, 49, 68, 114, 116
discrimination, vii, 45, 49, 64, 71, 82, 113, 115–16
  unfair, 114–15
disputes, 25, 45

di˙erences, 22, 98–99
Dominion Party, 42–43
Dorothy, 126–27
dream, 13, 32, 64
Dutch Reformed Church, 4–5, 63

E

ECC (End Conscription Campaign), 80, 87
economy, 4, 36, 41, 106, 108, 132
editor, 116
education, 12, 34, 62–64, 73, 94, 107–9
   children's, 86
   inferior, 64, 107
elders, 2, 16, 23, 27–29, 120
elections, 42–44, 76, 94, 111
Elizabeth, 127, 133
emancipate, 41–42, 103
Eminent Persons Group (EPG), 108–9
Emma, 11–12, 52, 89–94, 130
employers, 11, 61, 68, 90, 92–93
encouragement, xi
End Conscription Campaign (ECC), 80, 87
enjie, 13, 57, 95–100
enjiwe, 95–97, 99–100
enjiwe Mtintso, 56, 62, 81, 95
EPG (Eminent Persons Group), 108–9
equality, 29, 112, 114
ere, 7, 9, 15, 24, 49, 58, 75, 89–90, 98, 112, 119
European-African women, 76
European children, 108
European domination, 3, 35, 39
European groups, 34, 39
European hegemony in South Africa, 41
Europeans, vii, 17–18, 23–24, 30–31, 34–37, 39, 51, 56, 60, 72–73, 86, 125
European teachers, 70

European visitors, 25, 34
European women, 44
eviction, 45–46
e˙ects, 3, 52–53, 103, 110
e˙orts, 3, 10, 14, 44, 56, 62–63, 73, 83, 87–88, 90, 100–101, 108, 114, 118
   government's, 8, 86–87
   women's, 83
exile, 9, 12, 73, 76, 92, 98, 108, 126
expense, 6, 41–42, 69
experience, xi, 10, 12, 48, 52, 71, 78–79, 86, 93
Experience of Women Workers in South Africa, 123
exploitation, 7, 33, 68, 125
extinction, 38–39
ey, 6, 11, 19–27, 32–33, 35–36, 44, 46–47, 66, 68, 73, 80, 87, 92, 95, 102, 115, 117, 119

F

failure, 21, 45–46
families, xi, 2, 9–10, 13, 17–18, 20–21, 23, 25–27, 30, 33, 36, 44–45, 47–48, 52, 56, 60, 62, 66–68, 73–74, 79–80, 83–86, 93, 97, 100, 111
   extended, 29–30
   royal, 24, 61
   white, 69
farmers, 21, 23, 46, 65–66, 134
farms, 24, 35, 42, 46–47, 65–66, 116
fathers, 1, 10–11, 18, 23, 27, 29, 36, 67, 77, 86
Federation, 103
Federation of South African Women. *See* FSAW
Federation of South Africa Women, 8
female activists, 57, 75, 77

females, 17, 19, 24
Feminism and South African Studies, 124
Fight for Freedom in South Africa, 134
food, 22, 48, 69
forced removal, 52
Forced Removals in South Africa, 51, 131
formation, 75, 81–82, 91, 94
founding, 40–41
Freedom, 7, 63–64, 131–32, 134
Freedom Charter, 13–14, 112
freedoms, 3, 44, 66, 104, 113–14
FSAW (Federation of South African Women), 6, 8, 58, 74, 80–82, 87, 101, 112
FSAW Federation of South African Women, ix

G

gender, vii, 5–6, 44–45, 81, 105, 113–14, 116, 124–25
gender equality, 80, 105, 112, 116–18, 121
gender equity, 117, 120
gender inequality, vii, 26–27, 29, 118
gender issues, 117, 120
Gender Matters, 104–5, 116–19, 126
gender prejudice, 5–6
gender relations, 27–29
gender representation, 118
Getty Images, iv
gifts, 22, 29
girls, 18–23, 30, 46, 69, 126
God, 54, 113
God bless South Africa, 113
Goodman, 12, 57, 62, 68, 81, 96, 98–99, 126
goods, unload South African, 108
Goodwin, 5, 12–13, 95, 127

government, 8, 10, 13, 37, 42, 45, 50–51, 56–57, 60–63, 66, 70–71, 79, 84, 88, 104, 107–11, 113, 116, 118–21
government's decision, 88
government security agents, 9, 14
Group Areas Act, 13, 51, 59, 92, 110
groups, 13–14, 16–17, 19, 28, 34, 36, 39, 42–44, 54, 56, 66, 72, 76, 92–94, 98, 101, 109, 112, 118
anti-apartheid, viii, 110, 121
indigenous, 16–17
non-White, 5, 43
racial, 4, 54–55, 61
Growth of Peasant Communities, 61–62
Growth of Towns, 51, 53, 67

H

health, 34, 109, 111
herders, 16, 18–21, 23
Hertzog, 41–43
Hertzog government, 52–53
hinterland, 34–35
History, 22, 40, 82, 124, 128, 132
History of African People, 41, 49
History of South Africa, 13, 15, 17–28, 34, 36–40, 42–43, 55–57, 59, 62, 72, 76, 82, 106, 108, 110–11, 133
History of Southern Africa, 18–19, 21–22, 24–26, 28–30, 39, 41–43, 50–53, 56–57, 60–63, 131
homeland governments, 61
homelands, 30, 33, 38, 54, 60, 77, 107
homes, 1–2, 9, 18, 22, 27, 33, 38, 51–52, 66–67, 69, 73, 75, 86, 92, 111, 115, 121
Honor Women's Day, 75, 85–86, 88, 134
Hunters, 18–21
husbands, xi, 5, 16, 18–20, 28–29, 44, 47, 49, 51, 66, 73, 77–78, 85–86

I

ideals, 101–2, 112
   women's, 102
ideology, 54, 99, 126
ill, 10–11, 23, 34
implications, 2, 9, 18, 33, 40, 56, 64, 72, 108, 115
imprisonment, 8–9, 14
inability, 9
Indiana University Press, 123, 126, 129
Indians, 6, 70, 107
Inequality, 28, 118, 125
initiation, 1, 19, 21–23, 30
   female, 19, 23
initiation ceremonies, vii, 18, 20, 22–23
initiation experience, 19–20, 23
initiation process, 19, 21–23
initiation school, 19, 21–22
injustices, 91–92, 113
international pressures, 57, 111–12
interviews, 11–12, 54, 94, 119
Invention of Apartheid, 127
involvement, 20, 94, 108–9
   women's, 94
ird Edition, 129–30

J

jail, 8, 14, 86–88
jobs, 6, 59–60, 64, 67, 69–71, 94, 110
Johannesburg, 1–2, 7–8, 10, 28, 33, 49, 51–52, 58–59, 65, 68, 79, 91, 101, 125, 130–32, 135
Journal of African History vol, 123–24, 127, 129, 132
Journal of Southern African Studies vol, 125–26, 128, 135
judicial system, 25, 45
June Goodwin, 1, 28, 54, 56

K

Kagan, 91
Kgotla, 25
Khoi, 16–17, 26
Khoikhoi, 23, 35
Khoisan, 16–17, 26–27
killings, 84, 89, 106
Kinsman, 28–30, 128
Kinsman, Margaret, 15, 28
Klerk, 111

L

Labour Migration, 67, 127
land, 11, 27, 29–30, 44, 47–48, 54, 60, 65–67, 73, 80, 105, 111, 113, 119, 133
language, 100, 106, 114
late Black nationalist Steve Biko, 54
law, 9, 23, 25, 33, 43–45, 48, 52–53, 56–57, 60, 62, 67, 73, 77, 79, 82, 94, 112–16
   pass, 38, 53, 102, 107, 110
   rule of, 24–25
Lazar, Carol, 75–76
leaders, 21, 23, 26, 30, 41, 61, 83, 91–92, 96–98, 100–101, 119–21
   male, 9
   most secular anti-apartheid, 76
leadership, vii, 21, 24, 28, 81–82, 100
Legal Minors and Social Children, 45, 47, 131
legislation, 42, 60–62, 68, 82, 115, 127
Leo, 128, 130
Leonard, 13, 15, 17, 34, 76, 106, 133
Lesotho, 67, 97–98, 127
lessons, 19
level, 48, 66, 118
liberate, 94
liberation struggle, 3, 80
live births, 72

loneliness, 11, 49, 51
Long Walk to Freedom, 21–22, 25, 62–64, 79, 81, 96, 129

M

Mackay, Margaret, 77
Madams, 7, 33, 68–69, 125
maids, 7, 38, 46, 48, 73
Maids and Madams, 7, 33, 68–69, 125
Makhoere, 11, 53, 68–69, 129
Malan, 1, 5, 41–44, 54
Malan, Gabrielle, 1, 11
male relatives, 5–7, 30, 47, 51, 102, 119
malnutrition, 67, 71, 73
Mandela, 2, 5, 7, 9, 13, 21–22, 25, 112, 129
Mandela, Nelson, 2, 7, 22, 62–64, 79, 81, 85–86, 88, 96, 105, 109, 112
Mandela, Winnie, v, 2, 5–6, 10, 52, 57–58, 78, 81–86, 96, 99, 101, 120
Margaret, 125, 127–28
marriage, 2, 10, 19, 23, 29, 53, 56, 86
mixed, 1, 127
marriage ceremonies, 1–2, 10
marry, 24–25
Mashinini, 12, 52, 80, 89–94, 109, 111, 130
Mashinini, Emma, v, 10–12, 33, 51–52, 79, 81, 89, 108–9, 120
Mashinini's interview, 92, 94–95
Mattera, 79–80
McCuen, Gary E., 55, 62–63, 74
meid, 46–47
members, 10, 13, 16, 30, 40, 58, 73, 76, 80–81, 91–92, 98–99, 103
membership, full, 81–82
Men, 75
metropolitan regions, 110
Migration in South Africa, 124
minister, prime, 42–43, 74, 102, 110

minors, 9, 14
Mmanthatisi, 16, 29, 120
Molema, 29–30
money, 1, 33, 62–63, 65, 70
mortality rate, high, 72–73
Most women, 77
mothers, 1, 13, 18, 22–23, 46–47, 49, 56, 69, 78, 85, 87, 89, 98
mounting, 111–12
movement
  anti-apartheid, 87–88, 100, 109
  black trade union, 90
Mozambique, 35–36
multiracial democracy, vi, viii, 105–6, 112

N

Natal, 15, 39–40, 42–43, 128
nationalism, 44, 99
Nationalism in Twentieth Century South Africa, 129
National Union of Commercial and Allied Workers (NUCAW), 91
National Union of Distributive Workers (NUDW), 91
Native Administration Act, 52–53, 73
Native A'airs Commission, 50, 73
Native A'airs Department, 50
Native National Congress (NNC), ix, 40
natives, 7, 30, 34, 50–52, 60, 73
Natives Land Act, 40, 48, 72, 110
Nelson, 1–2, 10, 78, 83, 129–30
New South Africa, 7, 66, 76, 132
NGOs (Non-governmental Organizations), 117
Nguni, 25, 36
Nguni People, 17–19, 24, 34–35, 37
NH, 124, 131, 133
NNC (Native National Congress), ix, 40

NNC South African Native National Congress, ix
Nomazizi Sokudela, 80
Non-governmental Organizations (NGOs), 117
Nontsikelelo Albertina Sisulu, v, 81, 85
Normative Structure of South African Inequality, 4, 135
NUCAW (National Union of Commercial and Allied Workers), 91
NUDW (National Union of Distributive Workers), 91
numbers, 17, 40, 89, 97, 107–8, 111
large, 46, 106–7
nurses, 70–71, 83, 86–87
non-White, 71

O

Omer-Cooper, 18–19, 21–22, 24–26, 28–30, 39, 41–43, 50–53, 56–57, 60–63, 131
ompson, 13, 15, 17–28, 34–40, 42–43, 51, 53, 55–57, 59, 61–62, 67, 72, 76, 82, 106, 108, 110–11, 133
ompson states, 106
oppression, 6, 10, 56, 73, 76, 86, 99, 103–4, 116, 129
Oppression of Black Women in Apartheid South Africa, 71, 131
oracles, 20
ordeals, 10–11, 57
organizations, ix, 6, 41, 75, 80–83, 87–88, 91, 99, 102
o"ce, pass, 87
Oxford History of South Africa, 17, 22, 34–36, 39, 42, 51, 53, 61–62, 67
Oxford University Press, 17, 34, 130

P

PAC, 98–99
PAC members, 98
parents, xi, 10, 19, 47, 67–68, 84, 96
parliament, 40, 42–43, 110, 119, 121
participation, 4, 28, 104–5
women's, 102, 118
parties, political, 117
passive resistance, 7–9
Passive Resistance in South Africa, 7, 13, 81, 128
Paternalism, 65, 134
patriarchal system, 29–30
Peasant Communities, 61–62
Peoples and Policies of South Africa, 130
Perceptions of Apartheid, 132
permission, iv, 1–2, 26
Perold, 68–71, 94, 96, 98, 131
Piliso-Seroke, Joyce, 117–18
Plight of Black Women in South Africa, 45, 48–51, 65, 67–68, 70–71, 134
police, 11, 52, 97
police brutality, 52
policeman, 2, 58
policies, 6–7, 13, 42, 59, 63, 79, 107, 116, 130, 133
government's, 61, 63
Policy of Racial Segregation in South Africa, 128
political activities, 30, 87, 95, 98
Politics Protest and Political Transition in South Africa, 128
Port Elizabeth, 36, 110–11
Portrait of South Africa, 28, 49, 91, 131
Portsmouth, 16, 18, 124, 131, 133
post-apartheid situation, 14
post-apartheid South Africa, vi, viii, 3, 80, 103–5, 116–18
post-apartheid system, 112

power, 1–2, 6, 11, 13, 20, 28, 44, 59–60, 64, 72, 80–81, 95, 97, 107–8, 117, 126
  women's voting, 118
Power in South Africa, 126
power struggles, vii
power vacuum, 39, 41
preamble, 113
precolonial society, v, 18, 23, 30, 119
precolonial South Africa, v, vii, 15–16, 18, 23, 28–30, 105, 114, 119–20
Precolonial South African, 24
Pregnant Black, 71
President Nelson Mandela, 104
Pretoria, 4, 6, 8, 13, 72, 101
Prevention of Illegal Squatting Act, 60
pride, black, 96, 99
priests, 20, 91
prison, 8–11, 44, 58, 69, 76, 78, 83, 96, 101, 112, 129
privileges, 2–4, 24, 37, 60, 66, 113, 115, 119
problems, 9, 29, 33–34, 37, 49–50, 66, 68–69, 71, 75, 94, 118–19
process, xi, 19, 23, 35, 90, 92, 112
  decision-making, 110–11
Profiles of Leading Women, 75, 134
promises, 120–21
protests, 7–9, 13, 40, 74, 83–84, 89, 92, 97, 106
  anti-apartheid, 108
  anti-pass, 8
provisions, 60, 105, 112–13
Pty, 91, 131–32
puberty, 18–19, 21
punishment, 19, 46, 48, 71
Puri°ed National Party, 42–44

R

race, vii, 3–6, 44–45, 54, 77, 92, 99, 105, 113–14, 116, 118, 123, 125, 128–29, 133
racism, 4–5, 12, 113, 118, 120
racist system, 66, 72–73, 85, 106
rain-makers, 20
raising, 37, 46, 67, 73, 90
reforms, 109–10, 112, 125
refugees, 98
relationship, vii, 26, 45, 65, 85
relatives, xi, 5, 11, 45–46, 53
Republic of South Africa, 113–14, 125, 134
Reservation of Separate Amenities Act, 60–61
reserves, 40, 48, 50–51, 60, 67, 71, 73, 111, 120
resistance, 3, 13, 57, 61, 101, 104, 123, 126, 129, 134
  anti-apartheid, 3–4, 29
resources, 13–14, 30, 44, 61–62
responsibilities, 21, 36–37, 44, 46, 51, 84, 89, 97, 105, 115, 118
restrictions apartheid, 83
re‚ects, 13–14, 76, 100, 112
Rhodes, 32
richest, 24–25
riots, 84, 106
rituals, 24
rule, 19–20, 28–29, 54, 61, 71
Rural African Women and Taxation, 45, 47
Rural Women Join, 117
Russell, 7, 66, 76, 83, 85–87, 89, 91, 93–94, 96, 103, 132

S

SACP (South African Communist Party), 40, 80–81

SACP South African Communist Party, ix
SAIC (South African Indian Congress), 80–81
SAIC South African Indian Congress, ix
salaries, 70
San, 16–17, 23, 35, 37
SASO (South African Student Organization), 95
SASO South African Student Organization, ix
Saunders, 132
schoolchildren, 83–84
  unarmed, 83
schools, 12–13, 46, 59, 63, 68–71, 75, 84, 90, 106, 108
Section, 93, 114–15
security agents, 7, 11, 57–58, 78–79, 85, 97, 106
segregation, 51, 59, 110
Separation in South Africa, 133
servants, domestic, 44, 48, 61, 68, 70
service, 68, 70, 98
  domestic, 68–69
settling disputes, 25
sexism, 3–5, 12, 102, 113, 120, 132
  institutionalized, 118
Sharing Power & Decision, 118
sheep, 16–17, 25
sheets, 78
shootings, 83–84
Short History of South Africa, 133
sign, 96–97
silence, 19, 87, 89
Single Photograph, 75–76, 82, 129
Sisulu, 86–87
Sisulu, Walter, 85, 88
SMME in South African, 132
Smuts, 42–43
snake, 22–23
Social Children, 45, 47, 131

socialization, vii, 18–19, 25, 46
society, vii, 2, 4, 18, 21, 27, 29, 54, 68, 76, 94, 103, 111, 113, 116, 118, 128
  post-apartheid, 112
  traditional, 18, 20–21
soldiers, 38, 88–89
sons, xi, 16, 21, 27, 29, 36, 93, 98, 119, 133
Sophiatown, 8, 79–80
sorrow, 49
Sotho, 22–23, 25, 27, 29, 36, 120
Sotho kingdom, 29
Soul, 2, 5, 7, 9–10, 13, 52, 57–58, 78, 83–85, 96, 99, 101, 129
South Africa, vii–viii, 1–7, 9, 11–14, 17, 19, 21, 23, 25, 29–31, 33–45, 47, 49–51, 53–61, 63–65, 67–69, 71–75, 79–83, 89–91, 93–97, 99, 101–13, 115–21, 123–28, 131–33
  colonial, 38
  colonial/apartheid, 114
  democratic, 112–13
  history of, 76, 119
  independent, 40
  modern, 41
  pre-apartheid, 113
  rule, 5
South African, 3, 6, 10, 12, 14, 29, 35, 40, 49, 56, 67, 77, 101, 105, 108–9, 112–13, 115–18, 120–21
  native, vii, 24
  non-White, 8, 48
South African Activist Association vol, 126
South African and Namibian Liberation Struggles, 75
South African and Namibian Struggles, 134
South African Autobiography, 11, 33, 52, 79, 109

South African Black History, 132
South African Blacks, 66
South African Communist Party (SACP), 40, 80–81
South African Communist Party in Exile, 126
South African constitution, 112
South African Council of Churches, 76
South African Indian Congress (SAIC), 80–81
South African International, 130
South African land, 48
South African National Liberation, 126
South African National Liberation Movement, 6
South African Native Congress, 81
South African Native National Congress, 40
South African Parliament, 43
South African peoples, 112
South African practices, 54
South African Reserve Bank, 109
South African state, 57
South African Student Organization (SASO), 95
South African students, 76
South African War, vii, 39
South African Women, 1, 11, 28, 81, 95, 126, 129, 132
South African women of di erent racial/ethnic backgrounds, 6
South African Women's Resistance, 7
South Africa's land mass, 55
South Africa's World War II policy, 43
South Africa Women, 6, 64
Southern African Women, 123
Southern Tswana Women, 15
Soweto, 13, 57, 68, 83–84, 86, 95, 98, 106
sphere, public, 20–21, 26, 28, 116
sports, 62

spouses, 6–7, 67
state, 28, 43, 47, 114
staunch anti-apartheid activist, 86
Steve, 96, 98, 100
stock imagery, iv
street, 84, 92, 95
strengthen, 60
struggle, vii, 2–3, 6, 9–11, 14, 63, 75–78, 80–82, 85–86, 88–91, 94, 96–97, 99–100, 102–5, 120, 127, 130, 132
STRUGGLE, 3, 5, 7, 9, 11, 13, 17, 19, 21, 23, 25, 27, 29, 31, 33, 35, 37, 39, 41, 43, 45, 47, 49, 51, 53
anti-apartheid, 57, 73, 85, 103, 105
anti-colonial, 3, 121
Struggle for Freedom in South Africa, 132
Struggle in South Africa, 123
Struggle of Women in Southern Africa, 129
students, 95–96, 108
subjects, 7, 25–26, 28, 36, 43, 71, 115
Subordination of Southern Tswana Women, 15
Subsections, 114–15
Suppression of Communism Act, 13, 57, 87
supremacy, white, 41, 43
Surplus People, 51, 60, 131
Sweetman, David, 16

T

taboos, 23
Tamana, Dora, 75
Tambo, Oliver, 77
taxes, 47–48, 65, 119
    hut, 47
teachers, 23, 64, 70–71
tenants, 38, 65

displaced Black, 60
themes, 22, 114–15
Thousand Words, 75–76, 129
throne, 29
towns, 50–51, 53, 67, 79
trade unionists, helping Black, 93
trade unions, 10, 91, 102–3, 108–9
traditions, 2, 22, 24, 102
training, 71, 86, 95
transition, 18, 105, 112, 127, 129
Transkei, 13, 45, 47, 57, 61, 110, 131
trauma, 11, 79, 85
Treason Trial, 1–2, 10
Tripathy, 49–51, 64–65, 67–68, 70–71, 134
Tsonga, 22–23, 25, 61
Tswana, 25, 27, 36, 61
Tswana Women, 28, 128
tutor, 19
Twentieth Century South Africa, 129

U

UDF (United Democratic Front), 80–81, 85, 88
underpaid, 70–71
UNESCO radio, 96, 98
Union Laws on Black women, 18
Union of South Africa, 12, 40, 80, 82, 91
unions, 7, 12, 42, 90–92, 94
 a black shop-workers, 91
United Democratic Front. *See* UDF
United Nations Centre, 45, 75, 123, 134
United Party, 42–43
United States, 57, 107–8
University of California Press, 126, 134
University Press, 128–29
Urban Women, 127

V

Venda, 22–23, 25, 27, 61, 110

Verwoerd, 62–63, 70
victims, 6, 73, 84, 90, 93, 106
villages, 10, 17, 22, 25, 67
violence, 7, 52, 64, 74, 106
Vogelman, Lloyd, 74–75
voice, 6, 10, 12, 28, 82, 88, 90–91

W

Waldman, 45–47, 65, 134
war, 20, 23, 26, 37–39, 43, 89, 102
warriors, 21, 30
water, 19, 22, 101, 107
waterhole, 26
Welsh, 53
Welsh, David, 51–52, 67
White children, 68–69
White children's education, 63
White-controlled South Africa, 44
White employers, 7, 45–46, 92
White families, 61, 68, 73, 79
White farmers, 42, 45–47, 60, 65
White farms, 65, 67
White hegemony in South Africa, 5
White households, 7, 48, 68
White landlords, 45–46, 66
White minority government, 48, 62, 65, 72, 107
White minority government in South Africa, 53
White minority hegemony in South Africa, 13
White minority in South Africa, 45
White power, 13, 47
White Racist Rule in South Africa, 63, 130
White rule in South Africa, 5
Whites, 7, 40–41, 43–45, 48, 51, 53, 56, 72, 79, 106–8, 111
White schoolchildren, 62
White schools and Black schools, 111
White women, 5, 11–12, 42, 65, 72, 89

most, 89
protected, 6
White Working-Class Women, 127
Willen, Richard S., 4
Wilson, 17–25, 34–37, 39, 42, 51, 53, 61–62, 67
Wilson, Monica, 17, 34, 61
Winnie, 6, 10, 58–59, 78, 83–85, 87, 90, 100, 129
wives, 24–25, 27–28, 34, 46
women, vii–viii, 3, 5–9, 12, 14–16, 18, 20–24, 26–31, 33, 44–49, 51, 58–61, 65–67, 69–70, 74–77, 80–84, 86–87, 89, 94–95, 100–105, 109, 114–21, 123–24, 126–32, 134
   angry, 102
   classi°ed married, 9
   denied, 82
   ese, 7–8, 73
   excluded, 27
   experience of, 82, 119
   fellow, 100
   mature, 20
   native, 65
   non-Black, 11, 101
   non-European, 76
   rural, 117
   time, 20
   trade union, 87
   young, 49, 57
   young married, 49
Women, Davis A., 124
women activists, 82
Women and Resistance in South Africa, 61, 101, 134
women drift, cleaning, 68
womenfolk, 9, 103
Women in South Africa, 127
Women in South African Industry, 123
women in the apartheid society, 45
women leaders, 90, 101
Women Leaders in African History, 16, 29, 133
Women of Eastern and Southern Africa, 124
Women of Phokeng, 124
Women Rebel, 7, 134
women's activities, 102
Women's Charter, 101
Women's emancipation, 116
Women's Issues, 123
women's maternity rights, 94
Women's Press, 10, 129
Women's Press Ltd, 44
women's rights, 14, 116
Women's Struggle, 131
women's work, 69
Women Workers, 123, 131
workers, 65, 68, 76, 90, 92, 94, 108
   domestic, 33, 68
   social, 70, 84–85
Working Women, 28, 49, 68–71, 91–92, 94–96, 98, 131
World Rural Women's Day, 117
World War, 40–42
www.cge.org.za/about/vision.htm, 116

X

Xhosa, 13, 17, 24, 27, 36–37, 47, 57
Xhosa women, 36

Y

Yale University Press, 7, 13, 34, 76, 81, 106, 125, 133
Year of the Women, 77

Z

ZAR, 70, 84
Zindzi, 2, 78
Zulu, 36, 39, 44
Zulu army, 39